Ethelred L Taunton

The history and growth of church music

Ethelred L Taunton

The history and growth of church music

ISBN/EAN: 9783742861696

Manufactured in Europe, USA, Canada, Australia, Japa

Cover: Foto ©ninafisch / pixelio.de

Manufactured and distributed by brebook publishing software (www.brebook.com)

Ethelred L Taunton

The history and growth of church music

CONTENTS.

CHAPTER I.
INTRODUCTORY	PAGE 5

CHAPTER II.
STEPS IN ADVANCE	15

CHAPTER III.
PALESTRINA AND ORLANDO DI LASSO	24

CHAPTER IV.
THE SISTINE CHOIR	36

CHAPTER V.
THE TRANSITION	45

CHAPTER VI.
THE VIENNA SCHOOL	55

CHAPTER VII.
THE FOLLOWERS OF THE VIENNA SCHOOLS . . .	66

CHAPTER VIII.
THE LATER ITALIAN AND FRENCH SCHOOLS . . . 76

CHAPTER IX.
CHURCH MUSICIANS OF TO-DAY 85

CHAPTER X.
ON THE USE OF THE ORGAN AND ORCHESTRA IN DIVINE WORSHIP 95

CHAPTER XI.
ON THE PRESENT STATE OF CHURCH MUSIC IN THIS COUNTRY 106

CHAPTER XII.
CONCLUSION 119

APPENDIX.
A. AUTHORITIES CONSULTED 129

B. LIST OF MASSES 130

THE HISTORY AND GROWTH OF CHURCH MUSIC.

CHAPTER I.

INTRODUCTORY.

In presenting a sketch of the History and Growth of Church Music from the earliest times until the present day, I will endeavour to do so in a fashion which will consult the interest of the general reader rather than that of the specialist.

We will not pause to inquire what the church music was like in apostolic times; for hardly any trace of it is left beyond a few quotations from the sacred writings and other works which show, at any rate, that music *was* used in divine worship. It will suffice to recall St. Paul's words to the Ephesians, "Speaking to yourselves in psalms and hymns and spiritual canticles, singing and making melody in your hearts to the Lord;" and those of Pliny the younger, who, in writing to the Emperor Trajan (A.D. 110), speaks of the Christians as being in the habit of meeting " on fixed days before daybreak, and singing by turns a hymn to Christ as to a God." Whatever the music may have been, of this we can be sure, that from the circumstances in which the Church found herself—persecuted and obliged to hide from the face of day in the darkness of the catacombs— the means at her disposal for the celebration of musical services were of the simplest kind. The music was mostly congregational, for it was not until the Council of Laodicea (A.D. 320), that it was decreed "that no one must sing in the church but the canonical singers, who mount the lectern and sing from the book." And in the following century Pope Zachary in a letter to Pepin declared "that it was wrong for women to serve at the holy altars, or to take upon themselves any of the duties which pertained to men." Accordingly the music used in the Liturgy of the Church was rendered by clerics alone, who were at least of the rank of Lectors.

A rapid review of the relation of the Church in the earliest days to the arts, shows that the Church has all along pursued the same policy towards them as she did in the beginning. When the three hundred years of persecution were passed and the Church emerged from the catacombs, she began to present to the Pagan world the worship of the True God with all the majesty and beauty of holiness. She found ready to her hand a system of architecture, full of dignity and simplicity—a style in common and daily use. She took it and made it her own. In after years Catholic faith and Catholic genius invented another style in which were expressed the yearning of love and hope. This style, born within her bosom, the Church took up, adopted and used. She did not discard the older style, she kept and used it until it found its perfection in the glorious temple of St. Peter's on the Vatican. In the same way with the Gothic style of architecture; she nurtured this plant of her own growing until it reached its perfection at Cologne and Westminster. As with architecture so with painting and poetry. She "spoiled the Egyptians" of a style of art which was then in their possession; but within her fertile bosom new schools have arisen, which she has cultivated and cherished without discarding the old. And so, too, with the art of music. There was in vogue at that time a system of music, wonderfully complete and perfect of its kind—one which (and mark this carefully) the people were thoroughly accustomed to and understood—in fact, the musical vernacular of the day. This the Church took as her own and used in the services of her temples.

But at a later time and, curiously enough, about the same time as the Gothic style of architecture arose, there began to exist within the Church a desire for a further development of the art, and an endeavour to make of music an offering to God which would be more replete with the spirit of Catholic faith and love. And so in due course, after many feeble attempts at better things, a School of Music arose which—based, as was natural, on the old style—gradually emancipated itself until it gave to the Catholic Church the *Missa Papæ Marcelli* of Palestrina; and then, by a legitimate growth and logical development, Beethoven's *Mass in C.* This later growth in the Church has ever been watched over by her, cultivated and encouraged by her patronage, and used in her most sacred functions. Without neglecting the older style (or as much of it as has been preserved), which in certain cases she imposes as an obligation, and the use of which she encourages in every way, she takes its younger sister by the hand and offers before the Throne of God the choicest productions of the modern musical genius. Thus in all the arts the Church has taken from without what was at her hand, has used it and preserves it. But she has not bound her children down to that. She has not been barren but is made the "*Matrem filiorum lætantem.*" She has produced from within herself other works which are stamped with the mark of her divine beauty and bear on their face the sign of their origin. In this she has been like the prudent householder "who brings out of his treasures things new and old" that by so doing "she may give meat to her children in due season."

I now approach the subject of the earliest music of the Church, that is the Plain Chant, and in tracing its history, in spite of the eulogiums which have been passed upon it by its enthusiastic admirers (and they are often found to be gifted with more enthusiasm than knowledge) as to it being *the* music of the Church, and as to its heavenly origin, we are confronted by the fact that it is undoubtedly of *Pagan* origin. Some writers have imagined that Plain Chant is of Jewish origin and fondly fancy that what we hear in our churches are echoes of the old service of the Temple. But careful investigation has shown that, while there are certain points of resemblance between Jewish music and that of the Greeks (from which the Plain Chant is derived), yet the resemblances are of the faintest, and are no more than that likeness which the Greek music has to that of other Oriental peoples. But I would not venture to assert that positively no remains of the old Jewish music have, as it were, been translated into our Plain Chant; for the theory that some at least of the Psalm tones are substantially the same as were used in the Temple is not wanting in probability. But how far this may be the case I dare not venture to offer an opinion.

Now this Pagan music the Church took and used in her services, and in the course of years various psalms and hymns became identified with certain tunes. The first attempt to systematize the music of the Church was due to St. Ambrose, the great Bishop of Milan, who, towards the end of the fourth century, constructed what is called the Ambrosian Chant. We learn from a letter which he wrote to his sister, St. Marcellina, that his object was to regulate the tonality and the mode of execution of the hymns, psalms, and antiphons that were sung in his church at Milan. In order to attain this object, he took four of the Greek scales or *modes*, and rejecting their distinguishing Greek names (presumably to hide their pagan origin), he named them according to their tonal ascent—First, Second, Third and Fourth. It was according to melodies written in these modes that the psalms were sung, which, in time, made the Church of Milan so famous. St. Augustine, in his *Confessions*, speaks of being moved to tears by the beauty of the psalmody. It is difficult at this distance of time to discover what was the peculiar charm of the Ambrosian Chant, for I am not aware of any existing music which is Ambrosian, unless, perchance, it is the *accentus* (*i.e.*, the portions of the service sung by the priest and sacred ministers) of the Ambrosian Rite which is still used in the Duomo at Milan. But, still bearing in mind that the saint based his system on that of the Greeks, there is every reason to conclude that his melodies were of a similar character to that style, and would therefore be strictly metrical, founded on the syllabic contents of the text. This, I may say, is the opinion of the celebrated Guido of Arezzo. The Ambrosian Chant was, therefore, probably of a declamatory character, the melody being entirely subordinate to the words; and on this supposition it is not unlikely that the *accentus* of the Roman Rite (*e. g.* the *Preface* and *Pater Noster*) are of Ambrosian origin.

Nearly two-hundred years after St. Ambrose the work was

completed and made perfect by the great Pontiff Gregory I., from whose labours the Plain Chant takes its name of Gregorian. He added four more scales or modes to those fixed by St. Ambrose; and, calling the latter *authentic*, the new modes he called *plagal* or borrowed. For he borrows them, so to speak, by transposing each *authentic* scale a fourth lower, so by this arrangement the principal tone which formerly appeared as the fundamental or first note now appeared in the middle of the new scale. Among other beneficial changes we owe the system of the octave to St. Gregory, and also the modern names of the notes derived from the first seven letters of the alphabet. He used also a system of notation which is said to have been originated by St. Ephraim, and which consisted in little dashes, hooks, curves, dots and strokes, placed in all sorts of positions over the syllables of the text as a guide for the raising or falling of the voice. This system, known by the name of Neumes, was of its very nature uncertain; for the marks used gave no exact indication of the extent to which the voice was to be raised or depressed, and so we can feel for Cottonius writing four hundred years after, who complains that "the same marks which Master Trudo sang as thirds, were sung as fourths by Master Albinus; while Master Salomo asserts that fifths are the notes meant, so at last there were as many methods of singing as teachers of the art." It was not until the ninth century that the fact dawned upon some genius that a line, over and under which the *neumes* might be placed, would render less uncertain the position of the notes. This new departure was so successful that a second line soon made its appearance and was followed by others until the musician found himself with as many lines as there were notes! This was an *embarras de richesse* with a vengeance, but luckily Guido of Arezzo came to the rescue and simplified matters by reducing the number of lines, and placing his notes on the lines as well as in the spaces, thus giving us our present stave.

We must return from our digression on the history of Notation, and look at what St. Gregory accomplished. He collected the existing tunes, improved them and added many others. He then published the whole collection as a fixed standard to be followed by the Church. To attain this end (the uniformity of the Chant) he caused a copy of his work to be chained to the altar of St. Peter's so that it might remain there for ever as a reference and as the copy to be followed. In furtherance of his plan of reform he founded and richly endowed a School of Musicians in Rome who were carefully instructed in the manner of singing this Roman Chant; and so famous did they become that they were sent to various countries to introduce the true way of singing the Plain Chant. It was introduced into this country by St. Augustine; and in the seventh century we learn from the Venerable Bede, that St. Benet Biscop obtained from Pope Agatho the services of John, the chief singer of St. Peter's, to teach in his monastery the course of singing for the whole year as practised in Rome. So zealous was St. Gregory in undertaking this work of reforming the chant that, in spite of his bad health and the solicitude of all the churches which pressed heavily upon him, he used to superintend the training of the boys in Rome; and there used to be shewn in the Lateran Church the couch on which he reclined whilst directing the practice, and also (be not envious, O ye modern choirmasters!) the *scourge* with which he used to visit the faults and mistakes of his pupils.

The chant as arranged by St. Gregory differed from the Ambrosian in that it gave more attention to the melodiousness of the tunes and was no longer the mere slave of the quantity or length of the syllables. But, owing to the defective system of notation, and to the fact that the melodies came down by *oral* tradition, in course of time St. Gregory's work became obscured; and the state of affairs got to the pitch described by Cottonius, namely, that each master had his own way of singing the notes. Thus arose the various " uses" or local variations of the chant until, in the end, the exact original chant of St. Gregory was lost, and we can only guess what is the purest and most like the original. Much care has been spent in the last few centuries to remedy this uncertainty; and to no less a person than Palestrina was entrusted the work of purifying and restoring the chant as far as could be to its ancient form. He threw himself, with all his loyalty and devotion to the Church, into the work, in conjunction with his pupil, Guidetti; but death came upon him in the midst of his labours. From his papers, however, Guidetti completed the work as far as the *Graduale* and *Rituale* which were issued at the command of Paul V. from the Medicean Printing Press. He also brought out a revised *Directorium Chori*.

In 1848 the Abbé Voght and E. Duval brought out, at much cost and trouble, the edition of Plain Chant known as the Mechlin edition. The *Graduale*, though supposed to be based on the Medicean edition of Paul V., is not an exact reprint. Parts are due to the fancy and ingenuity of the editors; whilst in the *ordinarium missæ* they followed a local "use" of Antwerp. In the same way they have treated the *Vesperale*, which is based on, but is not a reprint of, an edition issued in Venice in 1650, and considered the purest form of the chant. The Mechlin edition, then, instead of restoring the chant as far as could be to its primitive form, has perpetuated the local variations which have crept in, and have been the overgrowth of centuries.

It is too modern; and it has destroyed the elasticity and suppleness of the chant, and what it has gained in sweetness, it has lost in dignity. After the death of Père Lambilotte, S.J., there was published, in 1857, from the papers he left behind, a copy of the famous Antiphonary of St. Gall, supposed by some to be an exact copy of the book which was chained to the altar of St. Peter's. But as this edition was only the result of the interpretation of the ancient neumes by the learned Jesuit, it was no sure guide. It was reserved to Pius IX. to initiate the desired reform, and to add another glory to his reign. As I have said before, it was impossible to know what was the exact form of the melodies as compiled by St. Gregory, so the direction in which the reform was to be taken was the reproduction, as far as possible, of the purest form of this chant based on the system of St. Gregory and purged of the growth of undue ornament which centuries had caused. The Pope entrusted the work to the Congregation of Sacred Rites, and a special commission was formed to take it in hand.

In his zeal for religion Herr Pustet of Ratisbon volunteered to place all the resources of his magnificent typographical establishment at the disposal of the Holy See, an offer the Holy Father accepted, granting in return a *privilegium* for thirty years to Herr Pustet.. The work of editing the choral books was entrusted by the Sacred Congregation to the Rev. Father Haberl, choir master of Ratisbon Cathedral, the most eminent authority on the subject of plain chant the age can boast. He carefully edited, in accordance with the rules and system of plain chant, and with German thoroughness and exactness, all the various volumes comprised in the series. The *Graduale* is a reprint of the Medicean Edition, and the Antiphonary is that of Venice, the music for the new feasts being supplied by Father Haberl. Each sheet of the first edition was sent to Rome and was submitted to the most rigorous examination by the Commission, and was then signed and sealed. And when in 1871 the magnificent folio edition of the *Graduale* was published by the authority of the Pope and under the direction of the Sacred Congregation, it came with the very same authority as the first book, chained by St. Gregory the Great to the altar in St. Peter's. In due time the other volumes were issued, and at length the great work is over, and we have a standard edition put out by Rome as containing the Roman chant. It is the desire of the Holy See that it should be everywhere adopted; in England the Fourth Provincial Council of Westminster ordered its use; and a degree of the S.C.R. renders its use compulsory in all future editions of the Missal and Pontifical. That is to say, the *accentus* of the celebrant and sacred ministers is to be in strict conformity with that of the Ratisbon edition.

Here I close this rapid and imperfect sketch of the history of Plain Chant. Imperfect though it be, it will suffice to show that, pagan as it is in its origin, it has been taken by the Church and made her own. The music which was understood and appreciated by the people was made an aid to them in their aspirations after the things of Heaven. That her policy is the same now as it was then, I will show in succeeding papers. As a lover of Plain Chant, who has spent years in its careful study, let me say once for all that, while I have no desire to see it usurp as of right divine the sole place in our choirs, I most earnestly wish its study to be promoted and its proper place vindicated; for I am confident that between, say, the *Missa de Angelis*, the *Missa Papæ Marcelli*, and *Beethoven in* C (these I use as typical examples of the three schools) there is no antagonism; but that all are treasures, new and old: the three Christian Graces—musical illustrations of Faith, Hope, and Charity.

CHAPTER II.

STEPS IN ADVANCE.

"LET us praise men of renown, such as by their skill sought out musical tunes and published canticles of the Scripture," who "set singers before the altar and by their voices made sweet melody, and to the festivals added beauty and set in order the solemn times." Prophetic words of Ecclesiasticus, and most truly applicable to the "men of renown" whose work I am going to trace!

We have now come to a period when men did not find in the Plain Chant adequate expression of the higher feelings which music engenders in hearts susceptible to its influence. It now began to be felt that music was capable of greater and better things than it had hitherto accomplished. Instead of being merely a melodious vehicle for the utterance of sacred words, it might be able to stir unknown and unsuspected depths in the human heart. It is noteworthy, as I have before mentioned, that at this period also in the sister art of architecture there began to be aspirations after better things; and this tendency was seen also in painting. Men had been satisfied with the solemn, simple, spiritual figures of Greek Art in the mere delineation of outline, but now the craving arose for the real. Men were of flesh and blood themselves, and they required that canvas which should appeal to them to be glowing with life. And as in music many attempts were made to add to melody other parts which should illustrate and accompany it; so in painting, perspective, colouring, and all the effects of light and shade, were introduced. Thus it came to pass that not many centuries after St. Gregory, men brought their skill to bear upon the Plain Chant; and, content at first with small beginnings, they gradually advanced towards perfection. Now begins the history of the second growth in Church Music, viz., that which sprang out of the Plain Chant and found the crown and perfection of its development in the Mass of Pope Marcellus. A third growth there was which came in with the use of the modern scale, and which is only a logical carrying-out of the principles animating the first writers; but at the present moment we will follow only the fortunes of the Polyphonic School, or the school of purely vocal music. It will be impossible to give more than a *resumé* of the work done by many of the "men of renown," so we will call attention to those only whose compositions make, so to speak, landmarks in history.

The first attempt, rude and bold indeed, made at harmonizing the Plain Chant was called *Organum*. We cannot tell when it first took its rise, or who was its originator. A clue, however, may be given by its name, which suggests that it may have come into use when the organ was introduced into the Church about the seventh century. As far as I know the earliest record we have of this kind of harmony is in the year 880, when in a treatise of Scotus Erigena we have a reference to it in such terms as leave no doubt that its use was quite familiar to those for whom he wrote. Now what was this *Organum* like? It consisted at first of the addition of a *third* to the last note of the Plain Chant so as to form a cadence. Delighted at this "new effect," the musicians of the day speedily added a *third* to each note of the Plain Chant. However, this was not looked upon with favour; and Hucbald, a monk of Flanders (930), gives us what is really the first intelligible account of the method used in the practice of what he calls organization. According to him, *Organum* consisted in the addition of either *fourths* below or *fifths* above the Plain Chant. The intervals of the *second* and *third* were only to be used when necessary to help the *fourths* to move more regularly. If any of my readers will play a simple piece of Plaint Chant over on the piano (say one of the Psalm tones), adding a *fourth* below or a *fifth* above the melody, they will obtain an idea of the hideous cacophony which delighted our forefathers. We admire their simplicity indeed; but I hardly think that even the ultrapurists of our day would advocate a return to the ancient method of the *Organum*. One of the very first rules we are now taught in harmony is to avoid the use of even two successive (perfect) *fifths* in similar motion; and here in *Organum* we have nothing else! *Tempora mutantur* may perhaps mean years change ears! By the way, it was customary for the Requiem Mass to be accompanied in *seconds*, the hideous discord being considered peculiarly appropriate.

However, *Organum*, much as we may now laugh at it, deserves our respect as a step in the right direction. Poor Music, the last born of the Arts, was still in leading-strings, and was just trying to walk; so we cannot wonder that its first steps were unsteady and shaky. But *Organum* led the way to a better state of art in the *Faux-Bourdon*, which arose in the 14th century, most likely at Avignon, whence it was taken to Rome at the close of the seventy years' captivity. The *Faux-Bourdons* consisted at first in the addition of a *fourth* and a *sixth* below the Plain Chant; and with the use continuously of the interval of the *third* (*i.e.*, between the *fourth* and *sixth*), the bass would sound a *false-bass* to those accustomed to hear only the intervals used in *Organum ;* hence its name. In time some of the new parts were sung *above* the Plain Chant. In the Sistine Chapel the custom of singing the Plain Chant in *falso-bordone* was kept up until the disbandment, after the occupation of Rome in 1870. These *Faux-Bourdons* gave an opportunity for a greater advance, and it was eagerly seized upon by the singers, who began to make the upper parts move with greater freedom. Hitherto all attempts at harmony had been in notes equal in length to the Plain Chant; but now, whilst preserving the same substantial harmony, the singers would improvise a part which, moving in notes of a different measure, was found to add life and grace to the general effect. This practice was called *Discant*, and the embellishments *Fioriture ;* and it rapidly spread over France where it first began, and thence to the Netherlands and Italy.

Though the *Faux-Bourdons* were a great development, yet they could not be called composition in its true sense; for they were only the enrichment of a given melody, with such harmonies as could be improvised at a moment's notice. Now composition is the *invention* of a certain definite musical idea, which the composer presents, now in one form, and now in another, until the discussion of its various qualities produces a work of art as thoroughly complete as a question in the *Summa*, or as a masterpiece of poetry or sculpture. A musical composition which is worthy of the name is as much the outcome of the exercise of the highest faculties of the mind and has to be as deeply planned, thought out, and carefully fashioned as any other work of Art. Between the tune discovered with the help of one finger on the piano, or the Oratorio which a certain popular author said he was sure he could compose if he only had someone who would take down the tunes he whistled whilst dressing in the morning, and a Mass by one of the great masters, there is as much difference as between a nursery rhyme like "Little Tom Tucker sang for his Supper" and the "Idylls of the King." Now composition dates from the rise of counterpoint, which consists in adding a melody or a number of melodies to some given subject with this aim—that, while each part or melody preserves its own characteristics and individuality, it forms a part of one harmonious design. Each melody springs from the subject, and exhibits it in its various lights, and, as it were, illustrates it; and in like manner it is related to the other melodies, sometimes by imitating a phrase appearing in another part, and sometimes by answering more or less closely some subject which has been proposed. Thus the parts go on interweaving and crossing one another, full of life and variety, yet all forming an orderly harmony. Such is the nature of true contrapuntal composition, and hence the name of the great school which excelled in its use, the Polyphonic or many-voiced school.

Like *Organum* and *Faux-Bourdons*, Polyphony was very gradual in its rise; and its earliest infancy has no record. This much we know, that Polyphony was systematically cultivated in Flanders during the latter half of the fourteenth century, and that the musicians of that country, if they were not the first to compose, were at any rate the first to teach us *how* to compose. The reputed founder of this new style of music was William Du Fay, a native of Chimay, who, after first practising his art with great success in his own country, went to Avignon and thence to Rome, where he entered the Papal choir as a tenor singer. He remained in Rome for the remainder of his days, working hard in the service of the Church; and when he died, in 1432, he left behind a number of disciples worthy of their master. Du Fay and his school delighted in taking some theme—a familiar folk-song—and developing it into a mass or motett for three or more voices. They had not a thought of irreverence in thus using a popular tune as the subject of their church compositions, any more than had the artists of the period who represented the Holy Family resting, during their flight to Egypt, at a Flemish hostelry. We may also bear in mind that most of the composers were churchmen of holy and spotless lives. The theme selected was generally sung by a tenor voice in long-sustained notes (hence the word tenor), whilst two or more parts played round it with an elaborate embroidery of counterpoint full of all sorts of musical devices. The Masses of the composers of this period are written in a hard, dry, and unmelodious style, with no attempt at expression. They were content with clothing the dry bones of the Plain Chant with a harmonious covering. It was reserved to a later time to possess the great gift of breathing spirit into the body and of bidding it stand up and live. But, taking these Masses as they are, we can recognize the great skill and earnest purpose of the masters. There is little regard for verbal accuracy or for distinction between long and short syllables. Sometimes, indeed, only the word *Kyrie* or *Sanctus* would be written as the beginning of a movement; and this was considered a sufficient guide to the composer's meaning. What unbounded confidence in the intelligence of his singers did not the composer show? but as he was himself generally one of the choir he was able to direct the performance of his work. The most eminent followers of Du Fay were Faugues, Redois, Eloy and Brasart, most of whom lived in Rome and were members of the Papal Choir. A valuable collection of their compositions exists in the archives of the Sistine, and we hope that facilities may be given for their publication; for at present we only possess some interesting fragments just sufficient to whet our appetites. It will be well to note how this new development was treated by the Church; how it grew up in and for her service, and how she used it for her public worship.

The next great name on the roll of "men of renown" is thet of John Okenheim, who, in 1443, was living at Antwerp. His style of composition was more elaborate and ornate than that of Du Fay, and there is no doubt but that the industry which he and his disciples displayed assisted the productions of a later time. Okenheim had great ingenuity in forming all sorts of puzzling musical devices, and he seemed to glory in doing his best to bewilder his performers. One of his masses, "*Cujusvis Toni*," demands, as its name implies, from the singers a thorough knowledge of all the old church modes, and a facility for passing from one mode into another. Yet although Okenheim, in his desire to astonish, often forgot the higher claims of art, he nevertheless taught his disciples an amount of technical skill which enabled them to overcome with ease difficulties otherwise insurmountable. He died at Tours in 1513, nearly a hundred years old.

We now gradually advance to better things. The dead body of music is beginning to stir with life; and the first to quicken it is the illustrious Josquin Despres. Baini, speaking of the state of music in Europe before the birth of Palestrina, says, "Josquin Despres was the idol of Europe. Josquin only was sung in Italy, in France and in Germany. It was only Josquin's music one heard in Flanders, Hungary, Bohemia, and Spain." He was a pupil of Okenheim; and he added to the wealth of learning he received from that master all the innate gifts of a genius. He brought greater freedom into his counterpoint; and, although his treatment of themes exceeded in complexity anything before attempted, his works are so endowed with life and vigour that even to our ears they sound strikingly effective and beautiful. Like almost all the great composers of this period, Josquin lived for some time in Rome (1471-1484, during the pontificate of Sixtus IV.), where he was esteemed the greatest composer the world had produced. He visited the Courts of Ferrara, Florence, and France, and left behind him many monuments of his skill in the Masses and Motetts he wrote for his various patrons. Many stories are told of him during his stay at the court of the French King, Louis XII. It seems that the King had promised Josquin some preferment. But the matter seemed to end there without prospect of the promise being fulfilled. Truth] to say, the King had forgotten all about it. But not so Master Josquin. He wrote a Motett to the words "*Memor esto verbi tui*" (Be mindful of thy Word!) and at the next great festival this was sung in the presence of King and Court. The King remembered his promise, and Josquin, in gratitude, wrote another motett to the words "*Bonitatem fecisti cum Servo tuo*" (Thou hast dealt kindly with thy servant.) Josquin, it would seem, was somewhat of a wit; but not always a reverent one. Indeed, the high quality of his work is often marred by this incongruous spirit; for sometimes in a single movement of his one finds, together with passages full of dignity and majesty, some quaint conceit and flashes of wit. But there are some of his works which breathe the very air of devotion, and it is in these that the name of Josquin Despres will live and be honoured. For instance, his *Stabat Mater* for five voices is a most pathetic and touching treatment of the hymn, and is surpassed only by Palestrina's wonderful setting of the same words. He is the first whose music has come down to us in sufficient quantity to enable us to judge of his power. We have in print nineteen masses—upwards of 156 motetts—besides a host of secular pieces. In all these we see a striving after life—an attempt to give expression to the meaning of the words. Burney calls him the "father of modern harmony." Be this as it may, he was undoubtedly during his life and long afterwards esteemed the most learned of musicians; and it is owing to this and to the just then introduced art of printing music by moveable types that we possess so many of his works. To sum up what has been said of this master we will quote the words of Ambros, the great authority on the mediæval composers:—"In Josquin we have the first musician who creates a genial impression." He died at Condé in 1521, just about the time of Palestrina's birth.

The earlier part of the 16th century gave us many writers, but they were mostly servile imitators of the great masters who had gone before. Venerable exceptions are to be found in the names of Carpentrasso, Morales, Goudimel (the master of Palestrina), Willaert and Festa, who, writing in a pure style, strove to beautify the body which their predecessors had created. We now approach to the two greatest masters of the Polyphonic School, Orlando di Lasso, and Palestrina the prince of musicians, contemporaries of each other. The one working in Rome, and the other at Munich, each surpassed all who had gone before; and so nearly attained perfection, as far as is given to man, that it is hard to say which excelled the other.

CHAPTER III.

PALESTRINA AND ORLANDO DI LASSO.

The illustrious Masters Palestrina and Orlando di Lasso are looked upon as the Saviours of Sacred Music. What, then, was the danger by which it was threatened? Nothing more or less than the total extinction of polyphonic music, and an enforced return to the Plain Chant. At the time of the Council of Trent there was a strong feeling against the use of figured music in the Church, and an attempt was made to forbid it altogether. But the wisdom of the Council was opposed to such a measure. "*Non impedias Musicam.*" But still the matter required reform, and reform was instituted.

Some of the causes of this feeling for reform have been hinted at in the former paper. They were chiefly these two. (1.) The composers of the age had forgotten that the aim of true Church Music was to produce in the souls of the hearers devotion and love, to awake echoes of Divine Faith and Hope. Forgetting this high end, they looked upon the Mass as a means of exhibiting their technical skill, and hence their productions were more calculated to astonish than to edify. The glory of God was nowhere; only the self-glorification of the composer was sought. The Sacred Text was but little considered, and was so overladen with ornament that no words could be distinguished. Church Music had ceased to be an art, and had descended into a mechanical display. A certain writer of the period, in speaking of the choirs of his day, says that the composers of Church Music were happy if they could make one voice sing *Sanctus* whilst another sang *Deus*, and yet a third vociferated *Sabaoth;* and then, in language not particularly elegant, he describes them as singing "with certain howls, bellowings, and gutteral sounds, so that they more resemble cats in January than flowers in May." When Nicholas V. asked Cardinal Capranica how he liked the singing of the Papal Choir, His Eminence said it was "like a sack full of young porkers, for he heard an awful row, but could not distinguish anything articulate." Clearly the time had come for the Church, as the true mistress of art, to interfere to save music from degenerating.

(2.) The next cause for complaint was the use which composers of Masses made of secular themes. These themes were often the tunes of lascivious and depraved popular songs; and the composers were not content with using the tunes, but often the very words, coarse and gross as they sometimes were, were sung by one voice to the original air whilst the other voices sang the words of the Mass. Those persons who are ready to imagine a state of affairs prevailing in our choirs similar to that existing at the period we are treating, would do well to realize that the strictures then applicable have absolutely no provocation nowadays. The nearest approach to it is a custom which, I regret to say, sometimes exists of adapting sacred words to some piece of secular music. Now this I most heartily reprobate, for it is unworthy of the Church, and is bad art; and where it is a case of some well-known secular air, it is a disedification to the Faithful. All introduction of secular music into the services of the Church is a grave error. The Church has treasures enough of her own, without having to descend to the opera or ball-room for her music.

The twofold reform to be made was that church music should be both suitable to the words and express their meaning, and that all secular themes should be banished. Thus the great principle of *dramatic* music was introduced, a principle which, from Palestrina down to our days, has animated all true Church composers. When I say *dramatic* music, I mean not merely descriptive, but also representative music. The Plain Chant did not aim at anything else than providing a more or less melodious vehicle for the enunciation of the Sacred Text. But, the growth of musical art had awakened new wants and new capabilities, and Sacred Music had to be brought into harmony with them. The use of the word dramatic in connection with Church music must not be thought out of place; for the most Holy Sacrifice of the Mass itself is the most sacred and high of all dramas. What does it in its outward form represent but the awful drama of Calvary? And as all the function of the Mass is dramatic and all its ceremonies are pregnant with holy meaning, so should be the music; and as to the extent to which the dramatic element is carried, I need do no more than refer to the singing of the Passion in Holy Week. The first striving, after better things has been discernible to us in the works of Josquin Despres; but the master who was to bring to the work the most consummate genius, as well as the self-abnegation of a true artist and an humble and devoted son of the Church, was the great Palestrina, the disciple and friend of St. Philip Neri, whose loving spirit his compositions reflect.

John Peter Aloysius Sante, called from his birth-place *Palestrina*, was the son of peasants in the Roman Campagna. According to the best authorities he was born in the year 1514, though Baini, his chief biographer, gives the date as ten years later. Of his earliest days hardly anything is known with certainty; but tradition has it that he was a chorister in the Church of St. Mary Major in Rome. In 1540 Palestrina entered the School of Music founded in Rome by Goudimel, and made such rapid progress, that four years later we find him appointed organist and choirmaster to the principal church of his native place. In 1548 he married, and his wife, whose name was Lucretia, bore him four sons, only the youngest of whom, Inigo, survived him. In 1551 he was back in Rome, and succeeded *Arcadelt* as Choir-Master of St. Peter's, at a salary of six scudi per month, a residence, and certain allowances. Three years were spent in quiet work, and at the end of 1554 he published his first volume of Masses for four voices, and dedicated the volume to Pope Julius III. In reward for this, the Pope nominated him one of the twenty-four singers who formed the Papal choir. This appointment, being more lucrative than that he was then holding, was gladly accepted. But it was not long enjoyed, for, by the Constitutions of the Choir, the members were required to be clerics, and to be able to sing, and in both these requirements Palestrina failed; for we read that as an adult he had little or no singing voice. So when Julius died, Paul IV., who began his reign by making numerous reforms, dismissed from the choir all those who had not the necessary qualifications, and among them Palestrina. The expulsion was softened down by a pension of six scudi a month; but still the effect was heavy upon the sensitive and highly-strung disposition of Palestrina, who took to his bed, and for some weeks was prostrate under an attack of fever. But Providence had not forgotten him, and two months after he was installed as Choir-Master to St. John Lateran, where he remained until 1561, when he accepted a similar post at St. Mary Major, remaining there for ten years, at a salary of sixteen scudi per month.

While at St. Mary Major, Palestrina achieved the great

work which, more than anything else, has made his name illustrious. In 1563, Pius IV. issued a commission to eight Cardinals, authorizing them to carry out the recommendations of the Council of Trent as to the reform of Church music. St. Charles Borromeo was the head of this Commission, and, being also the Archpriest of St. Mary Major, he was doubtless well acquainted with the extraordinary merits of Palestrina. St. Charles himself was a musician, and, as Cardinal Wiseman says, was "as true Saints ever were, a man of real taste." At his instance, and we believe at the instance also of St. Philip, Palestrina was commissioned to write a Mass which would satisfy the objections made against Church music, and would serve as a pattern to others. He was told that the fate of Sacred Music was committed to him, and he was urged to put forth all his powers. He accepted the task, but with a wise caution he would not trust the fate of his art to one work, but sent in to the Commission, for their approval, three Masses, each of them written for six voices—soprano, alto, two tenors, two basses. They were performed at the house of Cardinal Vitellozzi, one of the Commission, on the 28th of April, 1565; and although the first two gave great satisfaction, it was reserved to the third to win the enthusiastic approval of the Cardinals. The Pope ordered a special performance of this third Mass in the Sistine, and so delighted was he that he declared it must have been some such strains that the Apostle John heard sung by the Angelic Choir in the New Jerusalem, and that another John had caught and reproduced them upon earth. This Mass was shortly afterwards published under the title of the "Mass of Pope Marcellus," and is still admired by all musicians of cultivated taste.

A word now as to the form and style of this mass. What is known as the "Palestrina style" was not originated by the great master whose name it bears. What he did was to draw out to artistic perfection the rich legacy of counterpoint he received from his predecessors. But, as we have seen in the case of Josquin Despres, the uselessness and hindrance of mere technical skill when an appeal was to be made to the human soul had been discerned, and musicians were already at work on the true lines of art. Palestrina indeed surpassed them all, and by his compositions fixed and stamped a style of music which has since never been surpassed. This typical "Mass of Pope Marcellus" combines the highest skill in counterpoint (and one is amazed at the depth of learning and musical science which is displayed on its pages) with a close attention to the words and sense. I know no more tender and earnest pleading than the *Christe*, or anything more gorgeous or colossal in vocal harmonies than the *Sanctus*, a movement which is only approached by the *Sanctus* in Bach's B minor Mass. The delicious sentiment and refinement of the *Agnus Dei*, with its beautiful and mournful *Miserere*, is also noteworthy, but why select for praise one movement more than another when each page in this incomparable Mass is a triumph of Religious Art? Palestrina's Masses are not simple and are by no means easy, for they require the greatest care and the highest training that musical cultivation can obtain, and they are well worthy of all the trouble needed for their due performance. There is in them an intensity of human feeling which distinguishes them from all others of their style, and they are no less remarkable for their melodic beauty and the masterly management of the part-writing.

In reward for this Mass the Pope created the post of Composer to the Papal Chapel, and bestowed it upon Palestrina, and in 1571, owing to certain changes which had been made, he was re-appointed to his old place as Maestro in the Papal Choir, and also undertook the direction of the music in the Oratory founded by his friend and confessor St. Philip. Palestrina was most industrious, yet he had a hard task in making both ends meet. We see evidence of this constant struggle in a dedication of a volume of music to Sixtus V., which also reveals to us a sight of the man's interior piety and devotion to his art. "Holy Father," he writes, "study and care never consort together. To ask for more than a competency is to be wanting in moderation and temperance; having it, one may easily defend oneself from other cares, and whosoever does not has only himself to blame. But those alone who have had the experience can tell how hard it is to support oneself and family in credit; and how much such a necessity distracts the mind from the study of science and art, I unfortunately am but too well aware. However, I thank the Divine Goodness that, nothwithstanding my many great struggles, I have never ceased the study of music, but have always found in it a seasonable relief and distraction throughout the career I have run, and which is now drawing to its end. I have published a great many compositions and the printing of others is only retarded by my poverty, for the expense of printing such large notes and characters as may be serviceable for use in the Church is very great indeed." Worn out at last by age, he was attacked in the early part of 1594 by pleurisy; and, taking to his bed, he sent for St. Philip, in whose arms he expired on the feast of the Purification of Our Lady. His last worldly instructions were to his son, whom he ordered to see to the printing of his unpublished music for which he had enough money left. "I charge you," he said, "to see this done with all speed to the glory of the Most High God, and for the worship of His most holy Temple." He was buried, by order of the Pope, in the church of St. Peter, with all the honours and pomp used at the funerals of Cardinals and Princes. His coffin is laid in a tomb near the altar of SS. Simon and Jude, and bears the inscription: "Joannes Petrus Aloysius Prænestinus Musicæ Princeps"; and it is as the Prince of Music that his name lives in the records of fame. His Church works comprise 93 Masses; 63 motetts; the Hymns for the whole year, 45 in number; 68 offertories; 3 Books of Lamentations, and 2 Books of Magnificats. A complete collection of his music is now in course of publication in Germany, the first complete one which has been issued.

Whilst Palestrina was at work under the shadow of St. Peter's, another artist full of the same lofty enthusiasm carried on the same work at Munich—*Orlando di Lasso*, the glory of the Netherland School of Music, as Palestrina was of the Roman one. Space will not allow us to do more than give a very brief sketch of his life. Born in 1530, Orlando di Lasso (his real name was Roland de Lattre) first saw the light at Mons, and at the age of eight entered the choir of the church of St. Nicholas in that town. The boy was remarkable for the sweetness of his voice, and we learn that three times was he stolen away from Mons by agents who were on the look-out for voices for the private chapels of various princes. Twice his parents brought him back, but the third time, owing to a family disgrace he was allowed to stay at his own request in the service of the Viceroy of Sicily. He travelled in company with this prince, and devoted his time to the study of music, and seven years after, in 1551, we find him as choir-master at St. John's Lateran in Rome—at the time when Palestrina was occupying a similar post at St. Peter's. While Orlando was in the Eternal City he was living under the protection of our Cardinal Pole, by whom he was much esteemed. From Rome he passed to Antwerp, where, says a biographer, " he raised a taste for music, and gained the love and respect of the inhabitants." And all through his life we find that those who came in contact with him were won by his graciousness and sweetness of character no less than by his wonderful musical genius. In 1557 Albert V., Duke of Bavaria, invited him to his Court at Munich, and thither Orlando went and settled and married, spending there the remainder of his days, with the exception of a few visits to Paris. In 1562, to quote again the words of his biographer, "the Duke seeing that Master Orlando had by this time learned the language and had gained the good will and love of all by the propriety and gentleness of his behaviour, and that his compositions (in number infinite) were universally liked, without delay appointed him master of the chapel, to the evident pleasure of all. And, indeed, with all his distinguished colleagues he lived so quietly and peacefully that all were forced to love and respect him in his presence, and to praise him in his absence."

Here, prosperous and in a congenial atmosphere, he produced those masterpieces of Sacred music which have made his name immortal. He was ennobled by the Emperor; and from the Pope he received the Order of the Golden Spur. Princes vied with each other in conferring favours upon him, and his own sovereign had his works printed in the most sumptuous manner. Towards the end of his life his mind, owing to the unceasing strain of work, gave way, though death spared him for a while. His last days were sad, for he who had been the very soul of cheerfulness and brightness now became weary (*lassus* in name and nature) and mournful. When the end came he met death with Christian fortitude and resignation, and his last hours were soothed by the devoted attention and care of his loving wife and family. He died in June, 1594, six months after Palestrina had departed.

His compositions for the Church are marked by a great

simplicity, though at times he shows that he was not by any means deficient in the use of all the resources of his art. The style he used was of a grand and devotional nature, full of vigour, and yet abounding in grave delight. Every variety that can be obtained by natural modulation, by contrasted effects of repose and activity and by a skilful disposition of parts, are to be found in his works, and in hearing some of his masterpieces one is filled with a delicious sense of unworldly calm. The number of his compositions is said to be nearly 2,000, and include 50 Masses and about 1,200 Motetts.

Here, then, are the two great giants of music—" men of renown." We can see how they were both working for the same end, and it would be interesting to know how far the work of each influenced the other. In company with the two, we are first struck by their worldly position. Palestrina struggling against poverty and Orlando in wealth. We see in Palestrina *the* Church musician who wrote almost solely for the Church, whilst Orlando was more universal in his genius, although it is only in his capacity as an ecclesiastical musician that we here consider him. Palestrina was a genuine Italian, graceful, bright, soft, and delicately refined; and in his music we seem to see reflected the beauty and glorious splendours of the churches in Rome for which he wrote. All the wealth of imagination, all the delicacy of perfect form, all the richly harmonious tones of colours with which they are adorned, have their counterpart in the music of Palestrina. On the other hand Orlando was a German, cast in a simpler mould. He gives more attention to characteristic expression than to beauty of form, and, to keep up the architectural simile, when hearing Orlando's music we are no longer under the roofs of Roman churches, we are in the stately and majestic Gothic cathedrals of Germany. All around us is solid and massive, and breathing the spirit of mysticism. Another comparison between the two, is that Palestrina's music seems an echo of heavenly voices and is supernatural, whilst that of Orlando seems more that of the wayfarer still fighting on, full of hope, indeed, of the ultimate triumph, yet breathing the spirit of a true soldier of the Cross. The learned historian Ambros, says, " Palestrina brings the Angelic hosts down to earth, and Orlando raises men to heaven." The Italian master has been compared for his delicacy and grace of his style to Raffaelle, whilst the German master for his universality and the grandeur of his genius to Michael Angelo.

CHAPTER IV.

THE SISTINE CHOIR.

We have traced the growth of the Polyphonic School from its birth to its perfect development in the two great masters, Palestrina and Orlando di Lasso, and we will now examine the history of the famous Sistine Choir, for which so many of the masterpieces of this school were written, and which has preserved to our day the traditional manner of performing this music.

Let us go back in imagination twenty years. Let us take our way to the Sistine Chapel and listen to a service. It is Holy Week, and we are going to be present at the solemn office of Tenebræ. Having been duly provided with tickets of admission, we enter the Vatican Palace, and passing up the noble staircase, we come to the Sistine Chapel—a long, oblong hall of some 146 feet in length, by 50 feet in width. It was built by Pope Sixtus IV. in 1473, and its walls are decorated with the fresco work of Salviati, Perugino, Ghirlandaio, and others. Michael Angelo spent four years in decorating the roof, and also painted the famous "Last Judgment" which occupies the wall space behind the altar. The chapel is divided by a screen, and contains in the upper part the altar, the throne for the Holy Father, and the seats for the cardinals and other prelates. On the right, in a little gallery, is the place for the singers, who are hidden from view by a slight grille. The function is about to begin, the Pope is at his throne, and all that is high and dignified in the Church is gathered round about him. The perfectly trained singers of the Papal Choir intone the Plain Chant antiphons and psalms which are sung in a manner peculiar to the choir. Then after a pause there breaks upon the ear "*Incipit lamentationes Jeremiæ prophetæ,*" in the wonderful long-drawn harmonies of Palestrina. These are sung by four solo voices of the rarest beauty, and most beautifully do they blend, now rising in power, now dying away in the faintest whisper of the most plaintive and mournful cadence. As the voices float down the chapel the hardest heart must be touched and answers to the pleading call with which they all end: "*Jerusalem convertere ad Dominum Deum tuum.*" The second and third are sung to the Plain Chant melody, but with many a change and turn which are sanctioned by the use of centuries and which are valuable as relics of the old way of singing the chant. Then the rest of the service proceeds, and as we draw near to the end the attention of all is strained, for the far-famed *Miserere* of Gregorio Allegri will soon begin. See, the mystical lights are all extinguished save one, and darkness and gloom falls on the hushed crowd. One can just distinguish the colour of the Pope's vestments in the dim light, as he kneels in prayer. The *Benedictus* is over, and the clear tones of a soprano are heard singing, with exquisite feeling, *Christus factus est;* an awful pause, and then, like the far off echo of angelic choirs, there falls upon the ear the first sad wail, or rather heartbroken sob *Miserere,* and then it swells from the softest tone to a thrilling plaintive cry for mercy, and overpowers the hearers with the deepest emotion. Words cannot tell the effect of this matchless composition, so perfectly is it adapted to its surroundings and for the climax of the service. One must needs hear it either with the ears of reality or with the sympathetic ears of the imagination. There are many descriptions of this masterpiece, and I venture here to recall Cardinal Wiseman's, who describes it in his *Lectures upon Holy Week*. After having spoken of the first effect of the *Miserere*, he says, " here you can trace one part winding and climbing by soft and subdued steps through the labyrinth of sweet sounds, then another drops with delicious trickling from the highest compass to the level of the rest. Then one part seems at length to extricate itself, then another follows in imitative cadences, and they seem as silver threads that gradually unravel themselves and then wind round the fine, deep-toned bass which has scarcely swerved from its stately dignity during all the motion of the other parts, and fills up the magnificent diapason, and then the voices burst into a swelling final cadence which has no name upon earth." This is a popular description, and is strangely like one which Mendelssohn gives and to which we will refer later on. This *Miserere* is the composition of Gregorio Allegri, the last of the masters of the Palestrina School, and was for a long time most jealously guarded as one of the greatest treasures of the Sistine Choir, and it was forbidden under great penalties either to show or copy the music. The story of Mozart when yet a boy copying down the *Miserere* as he heard it sung during the Holy Week of 1770 is well known. In form this work is very simple. The first verse is sung to a figured chant for a chorus of five parts, which begins very soft and then swells out to a thrilling *forte* on the word *Deus;* the alto then leads off with a little subject which the other voices take up in imitation and break into a beautiful lingering cadence on the dominant. The second verse is sung in unison to the Second Tone, and four solo voices (soprano, alto, tenor and bass) sing the third verse and introduce in the middle and at the end the famous *Abellimenti*. These Mendelssohn, who heard them in 1830, describes in these words: "they are certainly not of ancient date, but nevertheless are composed with infinite talent and taste, and their effect is admirable. One in particular is often repeated and makes so deep an impression that when it begins an evident excitement pervades all present. The soprano intones the high C in a pure, soft voice, and allowing it to vibrate for a time slowly glides down, while the alto holds its C steadily so that at first I was under the delusion that the high C was still held by the soprano. The skill with which the harmony is gradually developed is truly marvellous." And so the verses go on with ever-varying expression and increasing effect until at last the voices join in a nine-part chorus and sing the final verse, getting slower and softer by degrees until they end, or rather extinguish, the harmony in a perfect point of sound.

The earliest records we have of a Papal choir go back to the time of St. Sylvester, who, early in the fourth century founded in Rome a School of Music for the education of Choristers; and in 580, the Benedictines, being driven out of their monastery at Monte Cassino, opened a school near the Lateran; and a few years later St. Gregory the Great used this school, which had increased in numbers, for the carrying out of the reform he had begun, and under his care so well did it prosper that, besides supplying singers who attended the Pope when he officiated, it was able to send out teachers to other countries which were desirous of being instructed in the method of singing the true Roman Chant. Other Schools of Music, sometimes called *Orphanotropia*, from the number of fatherless children they sheltered, having sprung up, were united by the Pope into one establishment, and were put under the care of an officer of high ecclesiastical rank who bore the title of *Primicerius*, and he was assisted by the *Secundicerius*, who exercised absolute control over the children. Boys were admitted at an early age, and if of noble birth, were made, at the same time, pages in the pontifical household. When their voices broke, they either were prepared for the Priesthood or became Chamberlains. The elder members of the Schola Cantorum, as it was called, had the title of Subdeacons; but this was only a titular dignity, for they were not allowed to exercise the office.

The next important change took place in 1305, when Clement V. went to Avignon, and left behind him his Schola Cantorum with their Primicerius. While the Papal Court remained at Avignon the music was conducted, with great magnificence, by a choir composed of twelve Choral Chaplains, who numbered among their body the most renowned musicians of the age, at that time mostly Netherlanders; and when we remember that the singers were also composers, we become aware of the talent and genius which were gathered together in the Papal Chapel. In the second of these papers we have seen how much the development and growth of music is due to the musicians of the Papal Chapel at Avignon; and so we are not surprised to learn that when, in 1377, Gregory XI. returned to Rome, he took with him his choir. The contrast between the old Roman Schola, which still existed and kept to the old manner of singing, and the New Choir, which had all the talent and cultivation of the age, was very marked, and great jealousy existed between the two bodies. But after a little while the Pope united them into one institution, under the name of the College of Choral Chaplains, and he appointed an ecclesiastic as their head, with the title of Master of the Papal Chapel, which office was borne for life. The first to enjoy this new dignity was Angelo, Abbot of S. Maria de Rivaldis, who held it in 1397. In the list of subsequent Masters we find no less than fourteen Bishops, the most celebrated of whom was *Elziario Genet*, called from his birthplace, *Il Carpentrasso*, made a Bishop *in partibus*, a very appropriate dignity for a composer of the Polyphonic School. He wrote some beautiful Lamentations, which were for a long time sung in Holy Week, until Palestrina's matchless compositions took their place. In 1586 Sixtus V. gave another constitution to the choir, and granted to the body the power of electing their own Master, who might hold the appointment for three, six, or twelve months, according to the will of the electors. The Master so elected was invested with all the dignities and honours of a Bishop, though, of course, not with the sacred character; and other Popes confirmed and increased these privileges. It was finally arranged that the election should take place each year, and the date was fixed for the 28th of December; and for many years it has been the custom always to elect the principal bass. There are many illustrious names connected with the Papal Choir as either singers and composers or masters. We have seen how the list was honoured by the name of the great Palestrina, and when, from force of circumstances, he was obliged to retire, the Pope gave him the title of Composer to the Papal Choir with a fixed stipend.

The number of singers was, as we have seen at Avignon, twelve. On the return to Rome, and the fusion with the old Schola, the number was raised to twenty-four, and was afterwards increased to thirty-two, which is now the normal strength, although, on special occasions, the admission of extra voices is allowed. The music which is composed by members of the choir, is, after it has been tried and voted worthy, copied in stencilled notes in huge books formed of whole parchment-skins, so large being the notes that the whole choir can read them at the same time.

Since the time of Palestrina but few changes have been made either in the character of the music or the style of singing, so the execution of the Sistine Choir is most valuable to us, as conveying a clear idea how the music of the Polyphonic School should be rendered. In the published Scores of that time there were no marks of expression used; all the devices of shading were left to the interpretation of the Master who directed the performance. That the music is not only capable of the highest use of the various means of expression, but that such expression is meant to be used, is clear from the traditions of the Papal Choir. We gather from these traditions the following hints for the correct performance of the Palestrina School of Music :—

(1.) It is quite a mistake to think that a large body of voices is necessary for the due rendering of these works. As we have seen, the ordinary number in the Papal Choir is thirty-two, in equal proportions of eight voices to a part. Indeed, in this kind of music the effect of a small, well-balanced choir is as great as of a large choir singing modern music; and this is accounted for by the life and motion of each part. It is hardly necessary to say that on no account are the voices to be accompanied by any instrument.

(2.) The pitch of the music may always be altered to suit the voices of the choir. For instance, the Mass of Pope Marcellus is too trying for the voices to sing in the original key, for our pitch is far higher than the old pitch of Palestrina's day; it is generally taken a whole tone lower.

(3.) As regards the time in which this kind of music is sung, it varies with the sentiments of the words and the requirements of the Liturgy, which have to be carefully studied by the choir-master. I refer here, for instance, to the words *Adoramus Te*, at which the sacred ministers are directed to bow their heads. The music here has to be sung slowly, so as to give the clergy time to uncover and bow their heads. The time of this style of music is, therefore, ever varying, and it calls for the most careful attention upon all who are concerned in the performance.

(4.) Every gradation in tone from the softest possible whisper to the grandest *forte* is needed during the course of a Mass, although any violent and sudden contrasts are out of place.

(5.) Various movements are given to solo voices whilst others are sung by the chorus, thus relief is given both to the singer and to the hearer.

(6.) The time should be beaten in minims, except in the case of movements in 3—1 time, when semibreves are the measure. In the Sistine the conductor marks the time with a roll of music-paper called the solfa.

(7.) There is a traditional way of bringing about crescendi and diminuendi which produces a result very puzzling to the uninitiated. The method is not only to increase the tone power produced by each singer, but also the actual number of voices used is increased for a crescendo and lessened for a diminuendo. The effect when carefully done is truly marvellous, and is capable of the most artistic results.

(8.) As a general treatment of a Mass we may note that the *Kyrie* is always sung slowly and devoutly with all possible shading; the *Christe* is similar time should be given to solo voices, whilst in the following *Kyrie* the chorus is again used and the time becomes a little more animated, though with a marked *rallentando* towards the end. In the *Gloria* the motion is quick and jubilant, but the words *Adoramus Te, Gratias, Jesu Christe* are sung slowly and very soft. The *Qui tollis* is a slower movement, and especial care is necessary for the *miserere* and *suscipe*. At the

Quoniam the original time is resumed with the exception of the *Jesu;* the *Amen* is drawn out until the sacred Ministers have reached the altar. In its general aspects the music of the *Credo* resembles the *Gloria*, but we often find the *Et incarnatus est* or the *Crucifixus* assigned to solo voices. The *rallentando* at the words *simul adoratur*, &c., must be marked, as also the final *Amen*. The *Sanctus* is always a slow and solemn movement generally sung with full power and strength. At the *Pleni sunt cœli* the time is generally quickened, and often the *Hosanna* is spirited in movement. The *Benedictus* is always given to solo voices and is marked with all the tenderness and grace which the singers can command. The *Agnus Dei* may be sung first by solo voices and then repeated in chorus. The time is like that of the *Kyrie*, and the movement needs the greatest delicacy of tone. I have given these few hints both because they may be of practical utility, and because they give us an insight into the meaning of the works of the masters of this school, and they show us how admirably the composers knew how to adapt their means to the end they had in view.

(9) An idea prevails that our modern choirs cannot sing Palestrina music, or rather that the *boys* cannot take the soprano parts. Now this is a great mistake, for the music was written in most cases for boys, and as we have seen, Palestrina himself was master of the choir boys of St. Peter's, and later on at St. Mary Major's. But towards the end of the sixteenth century the boys were supplanted by a new kind of adult soprano called the soprano-*falsetto*. They came originally from Spain where, by means of a peculiar system of voice training, the secret of which has never publicly been known, an adult was enabled to preserve in all its freshness his soprano voice. This result was brought about simply and solely by training, and travellers have expressed

their astonishment at hearing most beautiful flute-like notes coming from a big black-bearded man. We know something of this class of voice here in England where we employ the adult alto singer. It is the same kind of voice, but only trained and developed to the greatest perfection. In the seventeenth century another class of soprano came into use to whom we will do no more than refer. The (Spanish) soprano *arte fatta* is an exceedingly rare voice, and still exists, or did until lately, in Rome, and it is to be hoped that the system of voice-training which enables a singer to preserve by natural means the freshness and compass of his boy-voice, is not lost. What a boon it would be to choir-masters now-a-days, and only those who have known the disappointment of losing some beautiful voice from a choir by the breaking of the voice, can appreciate it at its value.

In concluding this sketch of the Sistine choir, we regret to add that it is now disbanded. The last day it sang in its official capacity was on September 8th, 1870, at the Church of S. Maria del Popolo. Twelve days after, Rome fell into the hands of its enemies, and the Holy Father became a prisoner in the Vatican. The Papal ceremonies of Holy Week are given up, and save at Consistories and at one annual function, the members of the choir never appear as a body. When the days of mourning are over and the Pope regains his freedom, then doubtlessly, the choir will be re-organised, and again set before the altar will they add beauty to the Solemn Feast.

CHAPTER V.

THE TRANSITION.

In taking up the history of Church Music after the death of Palestrina in 1594, we find that he left behind him many disciples who carried on his work, and who have left for themselves names illustrious in the history of the Art. Prominently among these figure the names of the two Naninis, of Felicio Anerio, of Vittoria, the composer of the well-known responses of the *Turba* sung in Holy Week; and of Allegri who may be called the last of the Palestrina school for with him this style came to a close. The great Master himself was the perfection and crown of the school, and his age saw the end of it, and the beginning of a revolution to which we owe the wonderful Art-creations of the present day. Polyphony had done its part, and, though the works it wrought will always endure as models of all that is refined and delicate in purely vocal music, it did not fully satisfy the want there was in the human heart. From its very nature polyphony was impersonal, and men were craving for the personal—for something that would be more real and a more faithful reflection of the sentiments which were within their souls. At this period (that of the death of Palestrina) all the Arts were feeling the effects of this fresh awakening; and the spirit of change which, in many cases, went to deplorable lengths, in music greatly benefitted the world.

So we have now to consider the Transition from the old Polyphonic school to the modern system of music. There were two causes for this transition—one, the introduction of instrumental accompaniment to the voices which had hitherto sung entirely unaccompanied; and the other, the development of solo singing, technically called Monody in opposition to Polyphony, and popularly Melody, for one or several voices with an accompaniment. These two causes worked together, and, though directed by different means, they both united in forming the modern subjective school. For the growth and development of instrumental music call for greater freedom than those laws of counterpoint which the Old Masters, writing solely for the voice, had considered necessary. For instance, many intervals which were difficult in purely vocal music, were found to be perfectly easy when they had to be played by an instrument: so why should Music be bound by laws which were of no practical utility? Thus the writers for instruments argued, and so the thin edge of the wedge was inserted, and with greater facility in the use of instruments came greater freedom from the old laws until the old edifice was tumbled down and a new one built up in its place. The old Gregorian scales, in which all compositions had been hitherto written, were abandoned when composers wrote for instruments; and the more perfect, because more natural and simple, modern scales came into regular use. They had long been used in the popular folk-songs of the day; and, although the practice of the schools was long opposed to them, yet when the wave of the Renaissance passed over the land the pedantry of the schools, which thought that without the Modes there was no salvation, had to give way to the demands of the new growth.

Again, it is undeniable that the practice which then arose of using instrumental accompaniment in secular music greatly influenced its introduction into the music of the Sanctuary, and here we see once more how the Church was ever alive to the ever varying wants of the age. What she did with the purely secular and pagan music in her early days, she did later on in the days of the Transition of music from the old to the new. It was her children who brought it about, and she fostered their work, and has given us, besides the treasures of Palestrina and Di Lasso, the beautiful art-works of Mozart and Haydn alive and glowing with modern life and spirit.

The whole school of Polyphony was, as we have said, impersonal; but when solo singing was introduced a more direct appeal to the heart was made and music became more the personal and individual expression of the singer who in music of the old school was only one of many. This system of Monody was due in its beginnings to a visionary restoration of the old Greek tragedy which then had sprung up in men's minds under the influence of the Renaissance. Palestrina, as we have seen, struck the key note of the dramatic principle; and in Monody we see the further growth of the same. The life and power of Monody lies in this, that it strives by its power of declamation to appeal at once to the heart of the hearer. The old school, as a whole, appealed more to the head and left the heart unsatisfied; and so Monody arose, and, defeating the old school, triumphantly established itself as master.

It is a grateful task to acknowledge that it is to one of the greatest saints of that age, to whom, in a large measure, the new growth of Church music is due. I am speaking of St. Philip Neri—a man of big heart, of artistic sensibility, and of unbounded knowledge of human wants. He saw at once what a valuable auxiliary instrumental music might be made in raising the mind to God, and so he seized it and directed towards the Sanctuary the stream which was daily growing in strength and power. In the services which he had established for young men in the Oratory, he alternated music with spiritual discourses; and, together with vocal music, he used such instrumental music as was then in vogue. Sometimes Sacred Musical dramas were performed, and hence arose those sacred quasi-dramatical compositions called Oratorios from the Oratory of St. Philip Neri. It was here, in 1600, that the first regular Oratorio was brought out. It was called *La Rappresentazione dell' anima e del corpo*, and was the composition of Emilio del Cavaliero, a Roman gentleman, and a Brother of the Little Oratory. Besides the fact of its being the first composition of a style which has given us the *Messiah* and *Elijah*, it is also remarkable for being, as far as we know, the first introduction of accompanied music into the Church, although not as yet into a liturgical service. Then another claim it has upon our regard—it is the first composition in which regular solo writing occurs. It was produced after the death of the composer, who, however, left very full directions as to the manner in which it was to be performed, and it came out ten months before the first opera was produced. Claims are made, and with a great show of likelihood, that Cavaliero has the honour of inventing the new system of monody. Be this as it may, we are certain that he was the first to make any extended use of it, and, moreover, was the first to introduce it into sacred compositions.

These were the lessons which the composers of the new system learnt from the revolution which was on hand. One was that voices, when they had the support of an accompaniment, could sing with ease many intervals which would otherwise be too difficult. This gave greater play to freedom of melody and execution, and the rapid strides which were made in the art of singing led to the establishment of a system of vocalization which is at the foundation of our modern school. Another lesson they learnt was that there were certain intervals which required instrumental support for their full effect, and this gave an importance to the accompaniment which saved it from remaining a simple background, and gradually brought it into the prominence and importance which the later masters have given it.

As in all revolutions the germs, as it were, of the change were floating about in the human mind, and there were many in whom the germs had taken root and had brought forth some fruit. But it needs a master mind who should gather up and collect all that was floating about, and start on a solid basis the new order of things; and in the musical revolution this master mind was found ready when most needed. Claudio Monteverde, who may be called the Founder of Modern Music, was born in 1568, and so was a contemporary of Palestrina. At an early age he entered the service of the Duke of Mantua as a Violist. He was instructed in counterpoint by Ingegnieri, who was a learned musician and a composer of some mark, and who held at that time the post of choir-master to the Duke. His pupil soon showed that he had no liking for the old scholastic music, and he bestowed no great attention on the wise saws and sayings of his master. Indeed, judging from a volume of madrigals published in his sixteenth year, which abounds in all sorts of musical profanities, we can imagine that Ingegnieri had rather a rough time of it, and that his serenity of mind was often disturbed by the disregard for the ancients which his pupil constantly displayed.

But in this and in some successive works Monteverde was only feeling his way; and when, in 1599, but five years after the death of Palestrina, he published another volume of madrigals, he was found to have cast aside once and for all the laws and trammels of the old school of counterpoint and to have entered upon a path which he not only pursued to his death, but which others have carried on to our day, and which lies at the foundation of modern music. Monteverde in 1603 succeeded Ingegnieri as choirmaster of the Ducal Court, and in 1613 he went to Venice in answer to a pressing invitation on the part of the authorities and here he became choirmaster of St. Mark's and gave himself up to the composition of Church music. His fame soon spread throughout the length and breadth of Europe as *the* musician of the age. He was one of the first who used instrumental accompaniment for Church music, and in a Mass composed in 1631 in thanksgiving for the cessation of the plague, we find in the *Gloria* and *Credo* a striking and effective accompaniment for trombones. Monteverde in his scores was the first to give to the violin its rightful place in the orchestra, and he is credited with being the inventor of two important devices of *tremolo* and *pizzicato*. In 1633 he became a priest and died ten years after and was buried in the Chiesa dei Frari. The greater number of his works have unfortunately been lost, but his influence upon music, and especially in regard to that division of the art with which we are here concerned, the path he opened has been trod by all the great masters who followed him, and his memory deserves our gratitude for opening to us so many beauties.

While Venice was thus at work under the influence of Monteverde in forming a new school, Naples was pursuing the same course under the Master Scarlatti, who was born in 1659 at Trepani in Sicily, and received his musical education partly at Parma and partly at Rome, where he studied under Carissimi. He produced nearly 200 Masses, which were greatly admired in his day; and we regret to say that only a very few have come down to us. Jomelli, one of the most illustrious masters of the new Neapolitan school, pronounces the Masses of Scarlatti to be the best he knew in the new style. But it was Leo, a pupil of Scarlatti's, who was the brightest star among all the new composers. He had a complete command of all musical science, and to that he added freshness of thought and striking originality. His music exhibits in a happy way the combination of the elegance and naturalness of the modern growth with the dignity and sublimity of the old masters. In Leo we seem to see the last farewell of the old musicians with all their breadth of conception and noble ideas; but although his harmonies are, in general, simple and clear, as the old masters loved, yet we sometimes come across chromatic progressions of a most startling character, while in his instrumental accompaniments his tonality is essentially modern. His Church compositions number about a hundred, and are of a very high quality. He died in 1746, and was the last of the grand Italian masters. In his day he saw the rise of what the Germans call Zopf, which is a term which is applied to all arts, and means a a predominance of the unreal—the incidental and external over the real, the essential and the internal. It is the confounding of the means with the end, an elaboration of one side of an art-work at the expense of all the others—a disturbing of the balance which should exist in all work which aims at the beautiful and harmonious. As applied to music it takes the form of mere display, or an elaboration of the melodic at the expense of the polyphonic and rhythmic elements of the art. Zopf, which means literally tuft, top-knot or pigtail, spread rapidly over Italy, and through all the countries of Europe in which the Italian influence existed. The generation of composers who succeeded Leo gave all their thought to the development of melody which should charm the ear, and with that they were satisfied and cared for nothing else. So one side of musical art was polished and cared for at the expense of all others, and the reign of the virtuoso was firmly established. It is curious to reflect that this state of deterioration and meretricious overgrowth had befallen the new school, when we remember how a like fate had befallen the Polyphonic School before Palestrina's time. I will leave it to others to philosophise about the causes, and content myself with stating the fact.

As the Polyphonic School had for its two great masters an Italian and a German, so it will be well for us now, leaving Italy for awhile, to see how the Transition effected Germany, and to trace its influence upon Church Music. The Transition did take root in Germany, but was not so revolutionary in character as it was in Italy. In the latter country, as we have seen, the old art was uprooted and destroyed; but in Germany the composers kept the old counterpoint, but, as it were, engrafted upon the old stock the beauties of the new style, thus keeping all that was good and real in the old and adding what was true in the new. And so it was that the two schools of music, the German and the Italian, have arisen, each showing the characteristics of the national character. Broadly speaking the Italian music is marked by melody, and the German school by harmony; and this is a natural result of the light and careless nature of the South as opposed to the studious habits of the North. Of course, this is only speaking in a general way, but a historical survey shows us that when Italy rejected counterpoint this revolution was never accepted in Germany, but together with the introduction of instrumental accompaniment and monody just so much innovation and freedom were allowed as were necessary for the full development of the new agents, while all that was not incompatible with the altered circumstances was retained, not only from a spirit of reverence for the past, but also from a conviction that it was of real and true value. The German masters did not destroy but they rebuilt upon the old foundation, they kept up all the learning of the schools and yet advanced with the times in all the new graces and elegances of musical diction. It is well to bear this in mind, as it explains the firm hold which the Church music which has come from this School has had and will have upon all lovers of true Church music.

Owing to the effects of the revolt against the Church, there is but little to record in the way of Catholic Church Music until the formation of the Vienna School of Church composers, about which we shall treat in the next paper. But we cannot pass over in silence the immortal name of John Sebastian Bach, who inherited the musical abilities and experience of a long line of masters. Little, however, can be here said of him, for his writings for the Church were few in number; but those which he did write are like his genius, simply colossal. Who has heard the glorious *B minor Mass* without emotion, and has not wondered at the overpowering effect produced by such apparently scanty means? From its length and enormous difficulty it can hardly have been intended for use as a Mass, but must remain, like Beethoven's *Mass in D*, in a class apart—a musical monument of the learning, power, and deep religious feeling of the composer. The sacred music of Bach with Latin words comprises the great *Mass in B minor*, four other Masses incomplete, and two Magnificats conceived on the grandest scale.

Of Handel, also, little need be said here, except that during his visit to Rome in 1707, besides two oratorios he wrote four Latin Psalms—a mottett—a *Kyrie* and *Gloria* and a *Magnificat*, and these he subsequently used as materials for his later compositions. All the German composers, although not writing for the Church, yet did good service in preserving the traditions of the old Polyphonic School, and so their experience was ready to the hand of Joseph Haydn when he came to teach the world how to combine the deepest science with all the warmth, life, and grace of Catholic love and the deepest piety.

CHAPTER VI.

THE VIENNA SCHOOL.

In treating of the Transition from the old school to the modern we spoke of the neglect of Counterpoint which had befallen Italy, and which gave rise to the degeneration of art and to the rise of the Zopf period. This Zopf never took much root in Germany, for there the studious and thorough character of the people inclined them to preserve the solidity which contrapuntal study gives. Yet they were fully alive to the necessity of making their art more a reflex of the emotions and sentiments of the human heart, and so we found them, while preserving the old, yet taking up and using all the graces and elegancies of the new school. In this they showed themselves true artists; for they gave their attention to the effect of the whole, and were not content with enhancing the beauty of one of the factors in their compositions at the expence of the others. They did not, as the Italian writers did, suffer the voice alone to predominate, just using the instruments as the merest background of sound upon which the senses might be supported. They made out of both voice and accompaniment a whole, the parts of which should mutually intensify and illustrate each other; and thus their conceptions were of a higher artistic nature, because more thorough, than those produced under the influence of Zopf.

In few parts of the wide domain of music was this influence of the German Transition felt more than in church music, and it is in the illustrious Vienna school that we find the happiest results. The masters of this school approached Church Music step by step with the advance of the modern science. They borrowed all the ease and freedom of melody, all the richness and variety of instrumental colouring, all the wealth of harmonic progression which mark the new from the old. We find in their sacred music infinite tenderness, all the graces of genius and all the intensity of imagination which one ever discovers in true works of art. To the hearer who understands the language in which they speak to the heart they are full of deep devotion, and now awake echoes of joy in the hearts of children rejoicing in the love of their Father, and now touch chords of heart-broken sorrow—a sorrow not of gloom and darkness, but a sorrow of wounded and contrite love. To understand them one must judge them simply from the warm Catholic idea of religion. Our service to God is not a recital of Commands intermingled with denunciatory preachments. Ours is eucharistic, and is as the Psalmist has it "the voice of rejoicing and thanksgiving, the sound of one feasting."

The father and founder of the Vienna school was the illustrious and immortal Haydn. Francis Joseph—so he stands in the baptismal register—was born in 1782 at Rohrau, a small Austrian village on the banks of the Leitha. He was the second child of his father, who was a master wheelwright by trade, honest and industrious, and above all a pious man, whose first care was to bring up his children as good, practical Catholics. Both the father and mother were devoted to music, and in such a congenial atmosphere the musical talent of the little Joseph, which had early shown itself, soon began to develop. As we are here concerned more with his works as a church musician than with his history, we will rapidly pass through the main features of his life. In 1740, Haydn entered the Choir School attached to St. Stephen's Cathedral in Vienna, and when his voice broke he was thrown upon the world with an empty purse and no friends. But friends arose, and though often in great need, Haydn was able to keep a roof over his head and to devote himself to the study of music. He eventually got introduced to Prince Esterhazy, who engaged him as Second Director of Music; and in May, 1761, Haydn set out for Eisenstadt, the country-seat of the Prince in whose service he passed the remainder of his life. The Esterhazy family were well-known as amateurs, and had at their country-seat a small but complete musical *chapel* as it was called, *i.e.*, a body of musicians, vocal and instrumental, who took part both in the church and in the daily concerts which were held for the recreation of the Prince and family. Here, at Eisenstadt, Haydn found himself appreciated, and on terms of affectionate intimacy with his princely master; and, under these circumstances, together with all the means at his disposal, his genius rapidly expanded, and he poured forth composition after composition. In 1766, Werner, the First Director, died, and Haydn succeeded to the sole direction of the music. In speaking of the circumstances with which he was surrounded, Haydn writes: "My Prince was always satisfied with my work. I not only had the encouragement of constant approval, but, as conductor of an orchestra, I could make experiments, observe what produced an effect and what weakened it, and was thus in a position to improve, alter, make additions or omissions, and be as bold as I pleased. Living in the country, I was cut off from the world and had no one to censure or torment me, and thus I was forced to become original." It was by these experiments that he invented the symphony, the instrumental quartett, and the sonata-form, all of which we owe to his genius; and besides these inventions in the form of music, Haydn is hailed as the Father of Instrumentation. In 1790 he went to live at Vienna, where he passed the rest of his life with the exception of two visits to England in 1791 and 1794. And on May 31st, 1809, he calmly died at the venerable age of seventy-seven.

Haydn was a most devout and practical Catholic, and looked upon his genius as a gift from above, for which he was bound to be thankful. Of his early days he used to say: "Almighty God, to whom I render thanks for all His unnumbered mercies, gave me such a facility in music that by the time I was six I stood up like a man and sang masses in the church choir." One is familiar with the story of the composer seated at his writing-table attired in full dress, saying his rosary in order to get inspiration. That is the idea of a Catholic artist sanctifying his work with prayer. On all his compositions are found pious inscriptions—"*In nomine Domini*" at the beginning, and "*Laus Deo*" at the end, and sometimes he added "*Beatæ Virgini Mariæ et omnibus Sanctis.*" In explanation of the great sense of joy and happiness which pervades his sacred compositions he said: "I cannot help it, I give forth what is in me. When I think of God, my heart is so full of joy that the notes fly off as from a spindle, and as He has given me a cheerful heart He will certainly pardon me if I serve Him cheerfully." And speaking of the time when he was writing the *Creation*, he said: "I was never so devout as then. Daily I prayed for strength to express myself in accordance with His holy will." These sayings reveal the whole heart of the man and show us the spirit in which he approached the work of composing for the Church, and so is it any wonder that his music has had a mighty effect in stirring up the devotion of thousands of Catholics and has led many souls to the true faith, drawing them by the cords of Adam?

His sacred compositions number fourteen Masses, a Stabat Mater, thirteen Offertories, four Motets, two Te Deums, a Tantum Ergo, four Salve Reginas, one Regina Cœli, two Ave Reginas, and the "Passion" or "Seven Words." A great number of other pieces are attributed to him.

The well-known Novello edition of Haydn's Masses does not follow the chronological order in which they were composed. His earliest Mass (Novello's Number 11.) was written about 1752, and about 1772 followed four Masses—one in G (Number 7), a particularly graceful and charming Mass, though marred by the Credo; one in C (Number 5); one in E flat (Number 12); and one in B flat (Number 8). His great Masses, known as the Esterhazy Masses, being written for the name-day of the Prince, comprise, in the order in which they were written, Novello's No. 2, called the "Paukenmesse," from the use of the drum at the "Dona"; No. 1, which will ever endure as a stately and majestic setting of the sacred words; No. 3, called here the "Imperial," from a story—since disproved—that it was composed for the coronation of the Emperor, but known in Germany as the "Nelson Mass," because it was performed during the visit of Nelson to Eisensladt in 1800, when, after hearing it, he asked Haydn for his pen and gave him his own watch in return; No. 16, in our opinion the finest and most masterly of all Haydn's Masses; Nos. 4 and 6. These Masses are all conceived on the largest scale, and are admirable for freshness of invention, breadth of design and richness of development, as they are for their scholarly learning and deep devotional spirit. They have won the highest praise of all musicians who understand the Catholic spirit of religion, and they have long held the foremost place in a choir where they are deservedly popular. Whilst lifting up the soul in prayer, they give also intellectual enjoyment of the highest order.

Mozart was born in 1756, and in 1781 fixed his residence in Vienna, where he continued to pour forth his soul in music, which has ever been the delight of cultivated minds, and which will surely endure in spite of the wild vagaries of would-be reformers. In spite of his fame the master had a hard struggle for existence; like many another genius he was very unbusinesslike, and was often in difficulties. He died on the 5th of December, 1791, but thirty-five years of age, and with strange neglect was buried in a common grave, the precise locality of which is unknown. He was a prolific writer, and besides the large number of secular compositions in every style and kind he wrote for the Church fifteen masses—two Litanies of the Blessed Sacrament, two Litanies of our Lady, two Sets of Vesper Psalms, a Te Deum, nine Offertories and many other shorter works.

It may here be remarked that it is somewhat, among a certain class of people, the fashion to sneer at Mozart as a Church composer, and it is said, that he was essentially an opera writer, and it was only the refuse of his genius that he gave to the Church, and also that he wrote for the Mass in a way he would have been ashamed to use in writing for the Stage. Now, these assertions are not only grossly false, but are also the result of ignorance and prejudice. For, as a matter of fact, what is the state of the case? He was in the service of the Archbishop of Salzburg as Music-Director, and in that capacity he had to provide music for the Church, and it was whilst he was at Salzburg that his church music was written. The operas which have made his name immortal as a dramatic composer, were written after he left Salzburg, and while he was living at Vienna; he did not write a single Mass to order, with the exception of the Requiem, which he left unfinished. We will bring Mozart himself as a witness as to his position as a Church composer. In applying for the post of Music Director he says of himself: "I have made Church music my *peculiar* study from my youth upwards." At Leipsic, in a conversation on Church music, Mozart said: "A Protestant could not possibly conceive the sentiments which the service of the Church awoke in a devout Catholic, nor could he understand the effect they had upon the genius of an artist." Writing for the Church was his delight, and to it he devoted all the fresh fervour of his early genius. And when in his last year we find him working at the *Requiem*, we see how he brought to his task all the power which experience and refined genius had given. The carelessness which is supposed to exist, but which we fail to discover, is certainly not apparent in his last work. It is all earnestness and deep reverential feeling. And the same vein runs through all his other works. What some might consider blemishes upon his works came from his position at Salzburg. There he was cramped and harassed by a tyrannical master, whose pleasure and gratitude Mozart never could win. But the best answer is his Church music itself. Of his Masses the best known in this country are (I quote Novello's edition) No. 1, a noble and highly dignified Mass; No. 2, a shorter but very popular composition; No. 3, a Mass of somewhat larger proportions, and one which combines, with a wealth of contrapuntal learning, all the graces of Mozart's best style; No. 6, a very graceful and melodious Mass; No. 7, a well-known and tuneful composition; and No. 10, which was a special favourite of Mozart's, and which is brimming with the most refined and graceful music. Of the Mass called "Mozart's

No. 12," I would say first that Jahn, the great Mozart historian, does not even mention this Mass among the compositions of Mozart, nor even among the doubtful works. Then it is generally attributed to Süssmayer, a pupil of the great master. Certainly, while on one hand we recognize much that bears the mark of Mozart, yet, on the other hand, there is much that is positively unworthy of the master. Weakness and padding abound, and besides, the fact that we find in Mozart's correspondence no hint of his being at work on a composition of such dimensions as this Mass, brings us to the conclusion that the Mass is not genuine, but that Süssmayer worked up into a Mass of his own composition sketches and hints for future use which he found among the papers of the master after his death. That he did so as regards the Requiem is a fact beyond dispute, for only as far as the *Lachrymosa* is the undoubted work of Mozart, the rest being either from sketches left or his own composition. It is, therefore, unfair to take the "Twelfth Mass" as being Mozart's, and on account of its many shortcomings to decry Mozart as a Church writer.

His Vespers are an elaborate setting of the Psalms for choir and orchestra, and abound in solid and majestical work. They take a very high place among his best works, and can be cordially recommended to choirs who are able to do them justice. The two Litanies of the Blessed Sacrament are characterized by great solemnity, and are full of passages of the greatest power and dignity. They would suit admirably for performance during such a solemnity as the Forty Hours' Exposition, and would be a valuable help in stirring up devotion in the hearers. His Litanies of Our Lady are elaborate settings of the Litany of Loretto, and are marked with the most tender love and grace. Of his offertories and motets we will only mention a "Misericordias Domini," which is written in the style of the old school, a "Venite populi" for double chorus, which teems with freshness and force, and the well-known and loved "Ave Verum," which certainly deserves the title of "Angelic." Poor Mozart has been badly treated by his friends, who have thus made themselves enemies. They have adapted sacred words to many of his secular pieces, and have palmed them off upon us as the genuine sacred compositions of the master. All this is bad, all this has done and does harm, and no one would have protested more energetically than the composer himself against this unwarrantable tampering with his works. The works which Mozart wrote for the Church are well suited for their sacred purpose; they were intended for that purpose, and we have seen how much Mozart esteemed his powers of writing for the Church. Let us be content with them, and not bring discredit both on the Church and on Mozart by these meretricious adaptations, which are both bad art and an injury to the cause of Church music.

There is one point in both Mozart and Haydn's Masses which demands a word—it is their frequent omission of words of the sacred text. This is, of course, unpardonable, and we cannot assign any reason for such carelessness. But in almost every case the words can be supplied by any choirmaster of average ability, and so the omission be made good. In the few cases in which the words cannot be inserted, of course those portions of the Mass in which they occur cannot be used.

The third great master of the Vienna school is the illustrious Ludwig Van Beethoven, the magnitude of whose genius has caused him to tower over almost all musicians. He was born at Bonn, on the banks of the Rhine, in 1770, and in his fourth year, according to his own statement, he began to study music. His father was his first teacher, and, being a hard, strict man, the little boy acquired his knowledge with many tears. At the age of fourteen we hear of Beethoven playing the organ for the six o'clock Mass every morning in the Church of the Minorites, at Bonn. After various changes we find him in 1792 settled in Vienna, where he remained for the rest of his life; and in the early part of his stay there he was receiving lessons from Haydn, and for over two years was under his instruction. We will not pursue his career any further, but just recording the date of his death, March 26th, 1827, will consider him in his works bearing on Church Music. .

Beethoven wrote only two Masses, one in C and one in D. Of the latter, the ripest fruit of his genius, we have already spoken. It is not a Mass in the usual sense. Both from its great length and inordinate difficulties it is quite impracticable for use in the Church, and so it stands, together with Bach's great *B minor Mass*, in a class by itself as a monument of the deep religious faith and highest musical gifts of the illustrious composer. His first *Mass in C*, written in 1807, for Prince Esterhazy, Haydn's patron, and first sung at Eisenstadt, on September 15th, is well-known and admired. In it the master seems to have summed up all that had been written by other composers. We find in it the dramatic element of which Palestrina was the pioneer, the grace of melody of Haydn, the refinement of Mozart—all meet here in this Mass in C; and through them all flows the originality of the master making it the richest and most glorious musical treasure the Church possesses.

These three masters—Haydn, Mozart, and Beethoven—the founders of modern music, are indeed typical Church writers. In their compositions we find the same principle which animated Palestrina, allowing, of course, a due development and growth. They are the true followers of the reform which he instituted; their music fills the void in the heart which he saw must be filled if music was to do its work. And triumphantly they have carried away the soul from thoughts of this world, and have borne it to the foot of the great White Throne. No one who is susceptible to the influence of music can hear one of these masses without being made better, and lifted at least for the time into a holier atmosphere.

CHAPTER VII.

THE FOLLOWERS OF THE VIENNA SCHOOL.

THE three great Masters, Haydn, Mozart, and Beethoven, have left their mark upon Church Music so strongly that the history of the Art from their day to ours is only that of the carrying out of the principles which guided them. The composers whose history, as far as it has to do with our subject, we are now going to discuss, were followers indeed of the Masters who had gone before, but they were not servile imitators, for they brought to their task all the originality of true genius, and, while following in the main the pattern laid down, their work is thoroughly characteristic of the individuality of each composer.

The first in order of time is John Nepomuk Hummel (born at Presburg, 1778, and died at Weimar, 1837), who had the inestimable advantage of being brought up in Mozart's own house, and so drank deeply of that Master's spirit. As a composer he was, of course, overpowered by the fame of Mozart, and had he lived at another time he would have most likely attained to a higher fame than he now holds. He possessed to the full every musical virtue —tasteful, refined, and elegant—but he is curiously devoid of originality in most of his compositions. But strangely enough his Church compositions are of a far higher order than his other works, and in them the Master seems to have put forth all his power. In one part of his career, from 1804 to 1811, he held Haydn's old post of music director to Prince Esterhazy, and it probably was whilst occupying this post that his Church Music was written. His Masses, three in number, are all conceived on large, broad scales, and can be classed with the six Esterhazy Masses of Haydn. The *Mass in D*, which is for chorus and orchestra without solo voices, is a dignified and jubilant setting of the words. The *Credo* is particularly fine, and in the *Gloria* the *Qui tollis* numbers as the finest movement in the whole Mass. The *Mass in B♭* is melodious and graceful, but perhaps wanting in power, whilst the *Mass in E♭* is worthy of one of the great Masters. I will only mention one movement, the beauty of which still lingers in my mind, although some years have passed since I heard it, the *Et incarnatus*, a most lovely tenor solo, full of devotion and reverence. Hummel also wrote two Offertories—one, *Quodquod in orbe*, a chorus with a very brilliant orchestral accompaniment, and *Alma Virgo*, for soprano, solo, and chorus. This solo is one of the sweetest in the whole range of Sacred Music, and is full of all that grace and beauty which Catholic composers seem ever to have when writing about our Blessed Lady. The difficulties of this piece, admirably written for the voice as it is, are very great, and demand great cultivation and power of execution on the part of the singer, and yet its fatal beauty has often tempted incompetent singers to try it with a result disastrous in the extreme. In the concluding chorus Hummel, for what reason we know not, introduces the melody of the threefold "Alleluia" sung on Holy Saturday. The three Masses and the Offertories are, as far as we know, all the Sacred compositions of Hummel, and their merits have won for themselves a high place in our choirs.

Franz Schubert, a real Vienna composer, was born in

that city, 1797, and there died, 1828, at the early age of thirty-one years. But in that short life he poured forth his soul in every kind of music in countless numbers; indeed, there is hardly any style of music in which he has not shown his power of excelling. He wrote a great deal for the Church, and as his sacred compositions are little known in this country, I feel sure that attention called to the wealth of beauty which is contained in them will be of advantage to those interested in Church Music. His Masses are six in number, and are all published in Novello's well-known octavo edition. Five of these Masses are published also by Augener, but as they reproduce the original text with certain omission of words, they are not of such practical usefulness as the Novello edition. The earliest Mass, the one in F, was written for the choir of the church at Lichtenthal, where Schubert as a boy used to sing, and which at this time was his resort on Sundays and Feast days. The Mass was written in 1814, when the composer was barely eighteen, and it is pronounced by a well-known and able critic, Mr. E. Prout, to be the most remarkable First Mass that has ever been produced, excepting, of course, Beethoven's *First Mass in C*. The Mass is brim full of the most delightful melody, and though, as was natural the influence of Haydn is apparent, yet there are passages, notably in the orchestral treatment of the *Kyrie*, which reveal the master-hand. The *Second Mass in G*, written the following year, is the shortest of his Masses, and like the First Mass was written for Lichtenthal. Short though it is, yet there is not a page which we could spare—indeed it would be hard to find any composition of the same size which contains so many beauties. The *Kyrie* is a smooth, graceful piece of writing, and contains an impassioned soprano solo for the *Christe*. The *Gloria* is jubilant and dignified, and conceived on broad and stately lines. The

Credo is a plain piece of writing; the chief interest is in the orchestral accompaniment. The *Credo* is remarkable, inasmuch as the music goes straight on without any break for the *Et incarnatus*. The *Sanctus* is exceedingly stately in form and rich in harmonies, while the *Benedictus*, written in the form of a canon for soprano, tenor, and bass, charms and delights the hearer, both as a worshipper and as a musician. A lovely melody, most daintily accompanied with ever varying figures, runs through the piece, and makes it the gem of the Mass. The *Agnus Dei* for solo voices, soprano and bass, is very beautiful, and the introduction of the choral *Miserere*, sung very softly, is exceedingly effective, and when, for the third *Agnus Dei*, the soprano takes up the original melody, but now transposed into the higher register of the voice, the impassioned pleading of the words is intense; and then, by one of those happy modulations of which Schubert is so fond, a return is made to the original key, and the *Dona nobis* is sung by the chorus in a peaceful and soft phrase, which, as it dies away, suggests that "peace which is beyond understanding." I have dwelt at length somewhat on this *Mass in G*, both because it is an especial favourite of mine and because it is a most useful short Mass, and one which should be in the repertoire of every choir capable of doing it justice. The third Mass is the *Mass in B flat*, written also in 1815, is well known and popular in Vienna, and is written in the master's happiest vein. The *Qui tollis* is a beautiful and dramatic setting of the text. The *Credo*, which is written as a plain *Canto fermo*, shows how much can be done by harmonic treatment and orchestral colouring. The *Benedictus* for solo voices is a melodious and almost heavenly quartette, and contains some beautiful canonic writing, whilst the *Agnus Dei* is indeed a delicate and charming conception, and is full of those touches of beauty which reveal the hand of a genius. The *Fourth Mass in C* (1818) is, like the other, full of beauty, and seems to show the influence of Mozart. And this seems more clear in the *Kyrie*, which some authorities go so far as to say might have been written by him. But the true Schubert is ever appearing in his own characteristic manner. These four Masses are all short, but are not easy. Besides good singing for the soloists, whom Schubert often takes to the highest range of their voices, the choral parts require great care and attention; but to a choir capable of doing them justice, the pleasure and delight they will experience in getting up these Masses will fully repay them for the necessary trouble. The other two Masses, the one in A (1822), and the one in E flat (1828), are conceived on a larger scale than any of his other Masses, and with the former Schubert never seems to have been satisfied for he was always making alterations. One of the most notable movements in the Mass is the *Gratias agimus*, in which, constantly, the word *gratias* is repeated by the chorus as though in the spirit of the deepest and unceasing thanksgiving. The *E flat Mass*, written during the last year of the composer's life, is a deep and serious work and bearing marks somewhat of haste, seems as though he already felt the hand of death upon him. Its great length precludes its use as a whole for church purposes; yet, although one is loathe to cut and interfere with a master's work, a judicious curtailment in the case of Schubert's music is not without its advantage. Indeed, the very exuberance of the master's genius sometimes calls for repression, and where used, as I said, with judgment and discrimination, the effect is often increased. Among his other sacred compositions I would mention a lovely *Salve Regina* for four male voices —a very gem of religious sentiment; *a Hymn to the Holy Ghost*, for eight voices, with an accompaniment for wind instruments; another *Salve Regina* for four mixed voices, and a *Tantum Ergo*, and a motett for four voices; *Benedictus es Domine*, a *Stabat Mater* in G Minor, a *Magnificat*, and a set of antiphons for Palm Sunday.

Carl Maria Von Weber (born 1786) wrote two Masses for the use of the Church—one in E flat, which is little known, and which is esteemed by musicians as a more solid and serious work than the popular setting in G. But in neither of these masses does Weber shine as a church composer. It was not his line, and the two Masses seem to have been experiments in this style of writing. They contain much that is exceedingly beautiful and worthy of its place, but the same cannot be said of the rest. We do not know of any other compositions by Weber for the Church, and this seems a proof that he himself recognized the fact that his genius did not lie in that direction. He died in London, 1826, and was buried at St. Mary's, Moorfields, and Mozart's glorious *Requiem* was sung on the occasion; and eighteen years after the remains were removed to Dresden.

Righini (born 1756, died 1812), a well-known musician in Berlin, betrays his Italian origin in his music. He wrote for the Church a *Te Deum* and a *Mass in D*, which latter work is full of pleasing passages of melody although by no means a serious and deep composition. A Requiem, I believe, completes the list of his church works.

Spohr (born 1784, died 1859) claims a word here for his *Mass à la Capella* for five solo voices, and give part chorus. A work which is full of difficulty, and the trouble needed for getting it up is hardly repaid by the results. It was recently produced in this country and failed to make much impression.

The Catholic compositions of Felix Mendelssohn Bartholdi (1809 to 1847) are so sound and beautiful that they make us regret deeply that the master was not spared to write more. But yet, as is natural, there is just *something* wanting in them which shows that they were written by one who was not a Catholic. This is apparent very much in the *Lauda Sion* in which we miss the tenderness and intimate love which would exist in one who believes in the Real Presence as taught by the Catholic Church, and who had been united in Holy Communion to his God and Saviour. This work, the most important of its kind composed by Mendelssohn, was written for Liege in 1846, and is well known at least in London where it is often performed during the Forty Hours' Exposition. It is full of dignity and majesty, and contains some of the Master's best writing. The lovely quartett *In hâc mensa Novi Regis* is a great favourite and most delightful to sing. In the choral *Docti Sacris* he uses the old Plain Chant melody with an elaborate accompaniment in florid counterpoint for the strings. The *Caro cibus* is a soprano solo of deep feeling, and the concluding chorus, *Bone Pastor*, dies away at the words *in terra viventium* as a far off echo of the land of the living. Three motetts for female voices—*Veni Domine, Surrexit Pastor, Laudate*, written in Rome for the nuns of the Convent of Trinità di Monti, are very beautiful works, and if only more known would be a very valuable acquisition to our convent choirs. A magnificent five-part chorus, *Tu es Petrus*, with orchestral accompaniment, and an *Ave Maria*, for tenor solo and double chorus are also greatly to be recommended. These compositions show us how Mendelssohn would have approached the subject of the Mass had he lived to have carried out the intention he had formed of writing one. It would have been written, in his own words, "with a constant recollection of its sacred purpose." But, as we have said, there is just that *something* wanting in his Catholic music which would have been there had he been a Catholic. It was to this that his want of understanding the gaiety and happiness of Haydn's Masses is to be attributed. It may be well here to mention that when in Rome he did not appreciate the Plain Chant even as sung by the Sistine Choir. In one of his letters he says, " It does irritate me to hear such sacred and touching words sung to such dull insignificant music. They say it is *canto fermo*, Gregorian, &c. No matter, If at that period there was neither the feeling nor the capacity to write in a different style at all events we have now the power to do so." To those who are fond of quoting the opinion of Mendelssohn respecting Haydn's Masses, in view of the above quotation I say if they will appeal to Cesar, to Cesar let them go, and I hope they will be satisfied.

Before closing the review of German Church composers, we must recall the memory of Carl Proske, who did so much for the recovery and preservation of the works of the Polyphonic Masters. He was a Canon and Choir-master of Ratisbon Cathedral, and in 1830 he began his celebrated collection of Church music. For this purpose he travelled for some years in Italy, and explored the MS. treasures which are contained in many of the great Italian libraries. He thus rescued from oblivion many most beautiful works, which he published in his well-known collection called *Musica Divina*, published by Pustet. This collection comprises Books of Masses, Motetts, Vesper music, Litanies and Holy Week music, and is brought out at a cheap price. It should be in the library of every choir of capability, and its treasures should be frequently brought into use.

Since the time of Proske, Ratisbon Cathedral has been the centre of what is called the Cecilian Movement, of which mention must be made in these pages. The founder of the Cecilién-Verein is a Dr. Franz Witt, a Bavarian priest of great learning and piety, and in 1868 he started the society, which as a pious good work undertaken for the glory of God, received two years later the blessing of the Holy See. There will always be men of the type of the *Laudator temporis acti*, who are so full of their admiration for the past that they forget the beauties of the present time. So while heartily in sympathy with the effects of the Cecilian Society for the revival of the olden music, and especially for the care they bestow upon the plain chant— efforts which are worthy of all praise, I cannot go to the length which they go, as is seen in the following summary of their principles, taken from the *Lyra Ecclesiastica* of January, 1884.

1. "The true music of the Church is the Gregorian Chant.

2. "Of all harmonised music approved by the Church and written in accordance with its Liturgy, the most ecclesiastical in its character is that of the Italian School of the sixteenth century, and best known as the Palestrina School.

3. "The florid style of so-called Church Music abounding in solos and torturing the liturgical words as exemplified in the more florid masses of the Haydn-Mozart School, is unecclesiastical in character and unfit for the Church's service.

4. "We approve of and warmly recommend the compositions of the modern Cecilian School which combine the traditions and spirit of the music of the ages of faith with the resources of modern music."

On these four heads we would briefly remark that the history of Church Music hardly bears out the statement of the first proposition; indeed, with the exception of the *accentus* in the Mass no special style of music is laid down as of obligation by the Church. The first of these papers, and indeed the whole scope of this history, is to show that the Church has taken up and used everything that is beautiful and true. To number 2, whilst treating the opinion of the Cecilian Society with all respect, the *consensus* of the whole world is rather against their position. But I shall have occasion in the chapter on "the present state of Church Music" to discuss this matter at greater length. No. 3 I can only stigmatise as a gross libel on the great Church musicians who are attacked, and as I have said before, springs either from the want of a due knowledge of the real reform which Palestrina instituted, or from the want of a capability to understand the meaning of these compositions. To those who can read history Palestrina, Haydn, Mozart, and Beethoven are all animated with the same principles and all worked for the same end. As regards No. 4 I cannot help saying that the modern examples of Polyphonic writing, with which I am acquainted, seem to me to be exceedingly dry and uninteresting. That wonderful life and "go" which mark the work of the Palestrina School is wanting in the modern writers. Whilst preserving the outer form they seemed to have failed in getting imbued with the inner spirit of these works. Truth to tell, the age of Polyphony is gone by. We do well to preserve the past and to use the treasures it bequeathed to us, but our creative powers do not run in the old lines, and it is useless to attempt to force the stream back into the old worn channel.

I have spoken thus about the Cecilian Society because it evinces a tendency to extremes, and in Church Music as in everything else, *in medio via tutissima*; and it is this mean that I am endeavouring to point out and make clear. It is, perhaps, though by the aid of such societies who run a theory to death that we are able to estimate the real value of their principles, and so fashion our course as to be both good and reasonable.

CHAPTER VIII.

THE LATER ITALIAN AND FRENCH SCHOOLS.

We left the History of the Italian School of Church Music at the death of Leo, and now following up its growth we come to the honoured name of Giovanni Battista Pergolesi, one of the particular ornaments of the Neapolitan School. He was born in 1710, in the States of the Church, and at an early age was taken to Naples and admitted to the Conservatorio dei Poveri in Gesù Cristo, as a violin student. He studied composition under Durante, and then under Feo, both learned masters of the old school, and under their direction he made rapid progress. But soon he shook off, to a great extent, the contrapuntal yoke, and wrote in a style which came more naturally to him, a style which was melodious and full of direct expression. He seems to have been a Little Brother of the Oratory at Naples, for during the time while he was at the Conservatorio he used to go each day to the Oratory to play an organ sonata or voluntary between the two discourses. His name soon began to be famous, and when, after a terrible earthquake, a mass of thanksgiving was ordered by the authorities, Pergolesi was commissioned to provide the music. He wrote for this occasion a Mass and vespers for two five-part choirs and a double orchestra, and subsequently he added parts for a third and a fourth choir. Leo was present at the service, aud was astonished both at the beauty of the work and at the short time in which it had been composed, and he publicly expressed the praise of the youthful composer. In 1734 he went to live under the shadow of the Holy House of Nazareth, at Loreto, and served the church there as choir-master. It was under the sweet influence of this holy spot that he wrote his well-known *Stabat Mater*, a beautiful and pathetic work for two voices (soprano and contralto), which was composed for the use of a Confraternity. It was his last work, for consumption had laid its hand upon him, and it was only with the greatest effort that he was able to finish it before the summons came which called him away at the early age of twenty-six. For the Church he wrote, besides the *Stabat Mater*, four Masses, ten Psalms, a *Salve Regina* (for voice, strings, and organ), which is accounted one of his happiest inspirations and is unsurpassed in purity of style and pathetic touching expression.

Of Zingarelli (born 1752, died 1837) little need be said here, but he claims a word as being the composer of the popular psalm, *Laudate pueri*. He was the chief musician of Naples in his day, and numbered among his pupils many illustrious names. The above-named psalm was written for the First Napoleon, and is a most melodious and joyful composition. Thoroughly Italian both in style and treatment, it bears the marks of one who thoroughly knew how to write for the voice. It was, I believe, the late Cardinal Wiseman who introduced this work into England, and since then it has ever been one of the most popular pieces in our choirs. The other compositions for the Church of Zingarelli are forgotten and are of little value. There are several adaptations of some of his secular pieces to sacred words, "arrangements" which are enough to show the want of good taste and sentiment on the part of the adaptors.

Of the early years of Rossini (born 1792, died 1868), there is hardly anything to record in the way of Church Music, with the exception of a Mass which he wrote in his seventeenth year whilst he was a student at the Liceo of Bologna, and which not satisfying him he tore up. In this we see a proof even at that early age of the view he held about Church Music, namely, that music intended for the use of the sanctuary should be of the very best that a man's genius can produce. It was, therefore, when he had attained the very height of his powers, and had produced his masterpiece *William Tell*, that Rossini turned his mind again to Church Music and gave us an art-creation of the highest beauty. I am speaking of the *Stabat Mater*, a work which, in spite of the abuse which has been heaped upon it from time to time by musical fossils, yet lives and gives pleasure and devotion to the thousands who can understand the work. It was begun in 1832 at the request of a friend who was anxious to serve the Spanish Minister, Senor Valera. When the MS. was sent to the Minister only six movements had been written by Rossini, and the other four were supplied by another hand. A condition was made that the score should not pass out of Valera's hands, and during his lifetime it was faithfully kept. But after his death the heirs of Senor Valera sold the *Stabat* to a Parisian publisher for the sum of 2,000 francs. Rossini was much displeased, and in order to protect himself took steps to stop the publication. He then composed the four movements which were wanting, and in 1841 the work was brought out in Paris amidst the greatest applause. Its brilliant success is the best answer to the criticism which has been passed upon it. To judge it properly one should remember, as in the case of Haydn, that religion to a Catholic is something more personal and intimate than it can be to any one else. Again, to an Italian there is no such thing as the mysterious gloom of religion. He lives in the full sunlight of Catholicism, and the supernatural is part and parcel of his daily life, and to no one is he more tender in his love, child-like and simple as it is, than he is to Our Lady. This, then, is the key to the understanding of Italian Church Music, and to the work in point—the *Stabat Mater*. An Englishman possibly would not have written a Stabat like Rossini's—most likely *could* not—but that is no reason to decry a composition because we are not accustomed to view it from the same point of view as the composer did. The reasonable way is to embue ourselves with his spirit, and then we can read his works aright and understand them, otherwise we are like, say, Englishmen who know only their own language, and who are so enamoured with their Shakespeare and Milton that they do not believe that there is any value in the works of others who have written in a language which they themselves cannot understand. As to the *Stabat Mater*, who can doubt the religious sentiment of the opening chorus, or the marvellous expression of which the *Cujus animam* (too often misinterpreted) is capable, the tenderness and pathos of the *Pro peccatis*, and the grandeur of the *Inflammatus?* These, and the unaccompanied quartett *Quando corpus*, will ever hold their place among the best works of modern Church Music. About 1847 Rossini wrote a *Tantum Ergo* for two tenors and bass, with orchestral accompaniment. This was written for the occasion of the re-opening of the Church of St. Francis at Bologna. A reverential and devotional setting of the first verse is followed by a brilliant hymn of exultation and praise to the *Genitori*, and is written in Rossini's best and happiest manner. An *O Salutaris* for four solo voices soon followed, and in 1864, in Paris, he produced, at the house of a friend, his "*Messe Solennelle*," an important composition for solo voices and chorus. At first written with an accompaniment for two pianos and a harmonium, Rossini afterwards scored for full orchestra. The *Sanctus* and *Agnus* are very beautiful, and the *O Salutaris*, which takes the place of the *Benedictus*, is an inspiration of ravishing beauty. The *Gloria* is considered the finest portion of the work, and the fluent style of the choral writing throughout is a surprise to many who look upon Rossini as but a shallow and artificial composer. In conclusion, we may say that, although Rossini cannot take rank as a first-class composer of Church Music, yet the work that he has done shows his great powers, and makes us greatly regret that he did not use them more for the glory of the Church.

We come now to one of the undoubted masters of Church music, and one whom we may look upon as the greatest Italian composer since the days of Palestrina. Maria Luigi Cherubini was born at Florence in 1760, and was the son of a musician; and according to himself began to learn music at six and composition at nine. His first work as a boy even was a Mass for voices and a band, and by his sixteenth year he had composed three Masses, four Psalms and a Te Deum, besides other works. When he was eighteen the Grand Duke sent him to Bologna to study under Sarti, and generously made an allowance for that purpose. Here the young musician acquired that contrapuntal knowledge which has made him master of his art. Few, indeed, have equalled him in this respect, and since his time none have excelled him. His compositions during his stay with Sarti are all written in the Palestrina style, and show that it was at the feet of that master that he took his lessons. But from 1780 all the church work seems to have stopped, and Cherubini appears to have devoted himself for over fourteen years to operatic writing, and after spending some years in travel he finally settled down in Paris. His health seems to have given way, and he retired to the château of his friend the Prince de Chimay and for a while gave up music altogether, and was absorbed in the study of botany. However, in 1809, towards the end of the year, a deputation from the neighbouring village waited upon him, and asked him to write a Mass for the approaching Feast of St. Cecilia. He refused; but his friends left music-paper in his way, and in a short while he began to sketch the outlines of his well-known *Mass in F* for three voices. He took to composition once more, and his main occupation for the rest of his life was composing works which will ever rank as among the richest musical treasures to which the Catholic Church has given birth. In 1816 he was appointed conjointly with Lesueur, " Musician and Superintendent of the King's Chapel," with a salary of 3,000 francs, and in 1822 he became Director of the Paris Conservatoire, into which works he threw all his energy. He lived in honour, position and wealth, until May 15th, 1842, when he died, greatly lamented as one of the foremost musicians of the day.

Besides the *Mass in F* and the youthful compositions, we have works written in the mature and refined period of Cherubini's genius—the *Mass in C*, a dignified and beautiful Mass, which should be a favourite with our choirs, and the *Mass in A*, written for the coronation of Charles X. in Rheims Cathedral. In writing this Mass Cherubini evidently had before his mind a stately and dignified ceremonial, and majesty and grandeur are marked upon every page. Broad and solid in structure, it is a noble specimen of Church Music, and may almost be classed with Beethoven's *Mass in C*. Indeed, it has been remarked "that in his artistic conception and interpretation, Cherubini shows an affinity to Beethoven, more especially in his

Masses." What can be grander than the *Gloria*, or what a more ideal interpretation than the *Credo*, or what more celestial than the *O salutaris ?* Then there are the *Mass in E* (lately introduced at the London Oratory), the *Mass in G*, and the colossal *Mass in D minor*. We have two *Requiems*, one in *C minor* for four voices and orchestra, full of beauty, touching pathos, and unutterable solemnity, and one in *D minor* for three male voices. This last was sung at the Jesuit Church in Farm Street in 1873, and made a deep impression. A competent critic says : " It is doubtful whether Cherubini's genius ever shone to greater advantage than in this gigantic work. Every movement is replete with interest, and the whirlwind of sound which ushers in the *Dies Irae* produces an effect which, once heard, can never be forgotten." Of his motetts it will be sufficient to call to remembrance that exquisite gem of devotional Art—the *Ave Maria*. Anything more charming, more pious, and more touching it would be difficult to find. Cherubini, besides the greatness of his own work, is remarkable for the influence he had on the Church Music in France. There, as a rule, the people had not risen beyond Plain Chant, but Cherubini gave an impetus and a solidity to the rising school of Church musicians, and his influence is still felt, and we may look upon him as the connecting link between the Italian and French schools. From under him, as Director, there passed out of the Conservatoire men who have had an undying influence upon the Art, and we are not going too far in saying that much of their success is due to the example and teaching of Cherubini.

We mentioned above, Lesueur as being, with Cherubini, the joint master of the king's chapel. He was born in 1763, and in his twenty-third year gained by competition the musical directorship of Notre Dame. Here he found the Chapter ready and willing to second his desires, and so he engaged a full orchestra, and gave magnificent performances of sacred music. His genius was great but was wayward and eccentric; still had it not been for the overpowering genius of Cherubini, he would doubtless have left a greater name. He held among other offices the Professorship of Composition at the Conservatoire, and had many illustrious pupils. One of his hobbies was ancient Greek Music, and with perfect seriousness he would expound to his pupils how one mode tended to virtue and another incited to vice. But, unfortunately, sometimes a mischievous pupil would mislead his ear by inverting the order of succession, and thus make the professor ascribe licentious powers to a mode he had before extolled as possessing the power of inciting men to virtue. This is said to have been a favourite amusement of Gounod, who was then a pupil at the Conservatoire. His sacred compositions number five Masses, three *Te Deums*, a *Stabat Mater*, several Psalms and Oratorios, and a great number of motetts. He died 1837.

Louis Niedermeyer (1802-1861), was a pupil of Zingarelli, and first tried his hand at opera, influenced thereto no doubt by his intimacy with Rossini, but his efforts were unsuccessful. His true genius lay in Sacred Music, and at length recognising this fact, he gave up attempting to write for the stage, and devoted himself to the service of the sanctuary. He formed a school for the study of Church Music, which we believe still exists, and bears the name of its founder. His great Mass with full orchestra is well known abroad, and certainly takes high rank as a work pure in style, dignified and melodious. Besides this he wrote numerous motetts and anthems, parts of masses for Low Mass, and he also started a periodical called *La Maîtraise*, specially devoted to Sacred Music, which ran for about four years. In 1855 he brought out a *Méthode d'accompagnement du Plain Chant*, which shows evident signs of hasty compilation, and on its appearance it was met with a storm of hostile criticism. Truth to say, he was not fit for bringing out such a book. Like so many plain chant enthusiasts of our day, he was sadly wanting in practical knowledge of the subject he was writing about, and therefore fell into many mistakes. But in modern Sacred Music he did good work, and his compositions will repay a choir-master for the time spent upon them. We must not measure his merits by the success he enjoyed, for they are far higher, but still his works will always hold an honourable place in Catholic Choirs.

There is not much more to be said about the past history and growth of Church Music in France, for in the past there was but little scope for Church musicians. Plain Chant reigned supreme in Lent and Paschal time, on Feast days and Fast days, and its monotonous strains supplied the music for the funeral as well as for the highest and most joyful occasion. The musicians had little or no encouragement from the French ecclesiastical authorities in the past, and so the history of French musical Art is mostly occupied with the stage, and name after name of composers who might have done so much for the service of the sanctuary attempted nothing, a result which we now deplore.

CHAPTER IX.

CHURCH MUSICIANS OF TO-DAY.

FOREMOST among the composers of Church Music who are making this latter half of the Nineteenth Century illustrious by their talent and genius there stands undoubtedly the name of Charles Gounod. He will be known to posterity mainly as a Church composer, and with the exception of his opera *Faust*, will hardly be recognized as having done anything else. Indeed the very success of this opera is due to the deeply religious and earnest sentiment which one finds in his Church Music, and we may say, without hesitation, that had the composer not been as it were, impregnated with the mysticism of the Sanctuary he could not have achieved so great a success with his opera.

Gounod was born in Paris, June 17, 1818, and his mother, being a distinguished pianist, took care that her little boy should receive at the earliest age the musical education of which he was capable. Having in due course passed through his classical education at the Lycée St. Louis, and taken a degree, he entered in 1836 the Conservatoire, and was placed under Halévy for counterpoint, and Lesueur for composition. In 1839 he gained the "Prix de Rome," and in accordance with the terms of the prize set out to Italy to study his art among all the glories of Rome. Here, his chief pursuit was the studying of the works of the Masters of the old historic Roman School, and notably those of their Prince, the immortal Palestrina. His first important work was a Mass, for three equal voices and orchestra, which was performed in 1841, in the French National Church, San Luigi dei Francesi; the MS. score he sent home, and it was deposited in the Library of the Conservatoire. This was soon followed by another Mass for three voices, without accompaniment, which was produced in Vienna, in 1843. His allotted time of study in Rome soon passed away, and returning to Paris he brought with him a strong leaning to Palestrina's music, and having drunk deeply of that Master's lore he has remained faithful throughout his career to the principles he then adopted as his own. When he arrived at Paris he became the organist and choir master of "Missions Etrangères," and it was whilst here that he came under the influence of the celebrated Dominican Père Lacordaire, who, with that peculiar fascination he possessed, had gathered round him young men of talent and genius, and was urging them to devote entirely to the service of God those gifts with which He had endowed them. Under this influence Gounod for a time gave his thoughts to the priesthood, and indeed in 1846 attended the lectures in Theology at the Seminary of St. Sulpice, as a preparation for entering upon the clerical state. But as with the Abbé Liszt, it was judged wiser for him to give up the idea of becoming a priest, and it was pointed out to him that his true vocation lay in serving the Church in a capacity which is only second to that of the holy Ministry. But the year of theological study had given him a love of reading which has never deserted him, and now, to this day, M. Gounod delights to quote the sayings of the Fathers, especially those of SS. Augustine and Bernard, who were his two favourites. It was about this period that he produced his well-known *Messe Solennelle* in G, which was the occasion of his first public appearance before the world, and strangely enough this took place in London, in St. Martin's Hall, under the direction of the late Mr. J. Hullah in 1851. The work gave rise to much discussion, but the opinion was unanimous, that in the composer there was found both a poet and a musician of a very high order. Most of his artistic life has been passed in Paris, with the exception of the first few years after the Franco-Prussian War, when he made England his home for a while.

Gounod's Church Music demands consideration. His first *Messe Solennelle*, "St. Cecilia," is well known and admired by all of correct taste. The *Credo* is often spoken of as being a model of what a *Credo* should be. In this and in, I think, all his Masses, he has given up the old custom of writing an elaborate fugue to the *Et vitam*, and contents himself with a short phrase of great melodic beauty often accompanied with the harp, as it were an echo of the life to come. I know of nothing more simple and more perfectly adapted to its place than the celestial *Benedictus* of this Mass. After the grandeur and glitter of the great and glorious *Sanctus* there is a solemn hush during the elevation, and then, sung out by a soprano floating on an accompaniment of divided strings, there breaks upon the ear *Benedictus qui venit* to a melody of the greatest simplicity, almost like a piece of Plain Chant. Simple though it is, in the hands of a good singer it is capable of arousing the deepest spirit of adoration in the heart of the worshipper. But it is hardly necessary to speak of this Mass as it is so well known in this country, and is one of the greatest favourites with our choirs. His second *Messe Solennelle*, known as the *Mass of the Sacred Heart*, is to my mind by far the finest of all his compositions, and is full of dignity and beauty. The *Kyrie* is a lovely piece of vocal writing and is built on the ordinary intonation of the *Gloria*. In this latter movement, after a pastoral movement for the orchestra with a persistent pedal note for the chorus, the *Laudamus* bursts out in fugal writing which is continued in an effective and broad style until the *Gratias*, at which point the music becomes softer although making up by degrees again to an effective close to the words "*Domini Deus.*" Another little passage of imitation of great beauty is given to the words *Domine Deus Rex cœlestis*, and the *Qui tollis* is carried straight through without any break. Mention must be made of the very effective and striking treatment of the *Suscipe*, which ends in a great cry for mercy. Of this fine Mass the *Credo* is the finest movement. Here we have a phrase of great dignity given alternately to the voices unaccompanied, and to the orchestra. After an *Et incarnatus* of great beauty with a wonderful accompaniment to the strings wailing and bemoaning the Crucified, we come to the *et Resurexit*—sung softly in two choirs, but gradually increasing in strength until the full power is brought out in the majestic *Et ascendit*, the pompous notes of the trumpets adding their brilliancy to the glorious tone picture of the description of the Ascension and the Future Coming for Judgment. But the *Benedictus* is to be counted the popular movement, and surely Gounod has never written a more delightfully melodious and graceful quartett than he has in this movement. It is for the solo voices and chorus, and is the only part of the Mass in which solo voices occur. The *Agnus Dei* is full of clever reminiscences of the *Kyrie* and is an equally beautiful number. This Mass is not much known in England, owing most likely to there being no English edition, it being only published in Paris. But as copies can be easily got through London firms, those of our choirs who have it not should speedily obtain and learn it, and great will be their delight.

The third *Messe Solennelle (des Paques)* bears marks of the oratorio of the *Redemption* upon it. It was written at that time, but it is not one of the master's best works, though there are some very beautiful passages, notably in the *Gloria*, with very interesting instrumental effects. For the Orpheonistes—a musical society of men—he has writen two Masses, one in C minor, and one in G. This latter is very good, although it cannot escape the charge of heaviness, which is inseparable from any continuous work for male voices alone. The *O Salutaris*, which, in accordance with French custom, is sung instead of the *Benedictus*, is very fine and beautiful. This *Mass in G* has been arranged by the composer for three female voices and so will be of use in convents, and in this form it is very effective. I have come across a short little Mass for two with an accompaniment for the harmonium. This little Mass, unknown, I think, in this country, was written especially for some nuns, and is easy and good. It lacks, however, the *Credo*. There is another Mass written on a large scale (though also without the *Credo*), the *Mass of the Holy Guardian Angels*. This was written for the Liverpool Festival, but seems to have dropped out of use, which is a pity, as some of it is remarkably good. The Mass is dedicated by the composer to our venerated Cardinal Archbishop.

Amongst his other Church Music we have an exquisite setting of part of the Lamentations, *Quomodo sedet sola civitas* for soprano solo, chorus and orchestra. A *Stabat Mater* and a setting of the Seven Words for unaccompanied chorus are well worth the attention of choirmasters on the look out for something for Good Friday. A beautiful and deeply religious setting of the *Ave verum*, written for Mr. Leslie's choir; besides several other settings of the same words, all of which are good. His fervent *Ave Maria*, founded on the First Bach Prelude, is well known and admired. But it is impossible to mention all his sacred works for there is hardly any part of Church Music which he has not made the richer by his compositions.

His Oratorios, true Church compositions, are three in number. One, *Tobias*, about which I must confess utter ignorance. *The Redemption*, which is a touching and reverent musical treatise *de Deo Redemptore*, and which is marked "Catholic" on every page; and his last great work, dedicated to the Holy Father, *Mors et Vita*, consisting of a Requiem Mass for the first part, and extracts from the Apocalypse of the Future life. The proper place for these oratorios is the Church. Deep, serious, and religious, full of beauty, pathos, and dignity, they seem to call for the sacred surroundings of a church, and are out of place in the glitter and glare of the concert room. It was with pleasure that I noted a few weeks ago, that the Most Rev. Dr. Donnelly, Bishop of Cannea, had a performance of the last-named oratorio in his church near Dublin, and the performance, which was attended by His Grace the Most Rev. Dr. Walsh, made a deep impression on all those who were present. The Church was the cradle of the oratorio, and it is a great pity that we do not have more opportunities of hearing the great masterpieces of Catholic art (and all good art is Catholic) in their natural home.

Little has been done in this country for the advancement of Church Music, owing doubtless to the poverty of our Churches. But with the other beauties of the Second Spring, Church Music has developed, and now we have in our midst musicians of whom we may well be proud, though, I am sorry to say, their merits are not known as they should be, nor their works as extensively used as they deserve.

Edward Silas, a pupil of the Paris Conservatoire, has since his residence in England, now for nearly forty years, enriched our store of Church Music by a noble *Mass in C*, which deserves the highest commendation. This Mass gained the prize over sixty others in a competition held in Belgium in 1866. The *Kyrie* is evidently built upon the model of *Beethoven's Mass in C*, and is a capital piece of writing. One is struck by the bold and dignified treatment of the *Gloria*, and in the *Credo* the impression is deepened, a persistent orchestral figure in the first movement giving great character and force. In this Mass is included a remarkably graceful duet for soprano and alto with chorus —an *Ave Maria*. For a long time M. Silas has been organist and choirmaster at Kingston-on-Thames, and has written a large number of pieces of sacred music. A fine *Magnificat* conceived upon a large scale, and full of beauty, an *O Salutaris* and *Tantum Ergo* very devotional and good, and several motetts also bear witness to the great capabilities of the composer. Indeed, M. Silas has the reputation of being the best master of counterpoint in Europe, and his sacred works show the master hand at its best.

Another name of which we may be proud is that of Thomas Wingham, the Director of the London Oratory Choir. The favourite pupil of the late Sir W. Sterndale Bennett, the greatest English musician, Mr. Wingham has added to the delicacy and grace of his own genius much of the refinement and exquisite polish of his master. Writing on the classical models, Mr. Wingham has produced church compositions full of power and originality. A very fine *Mass in D* written in 1876 for the Cathedral at Antwerp is worthy of all attention. The *Kyrie*, a movement in $\frac{2}{4}$ time, is very good, and has a passage of great power for the *Christe*. There is a delicious little phrase for the oboe solo accompanying the repetition of the word *Kyrie*, and a gradual crescendo upon a long pedal works up the movement to a striking forte, which then gradually sinks down softly again to the end. The *Gloria*, for chorus and orchestra, is brilliant and bold in its treatment and is full of beautiful passages, whilst in the *Qui tollis* we have the solo voices used with effect. The *Cum Sancto Spiritu* is a well-developed fugue as full of life and power as any of the old standard Masses, and Mr. Wingham has proved himself not a servile imitator of the old classical school, but a musician who can think for himself and impress upon his work his own individuality. The *Credo* is quite in keeping with the high mark of excellence to which the whole Mass attains. The *Crucifixus* calls for attention for its striking originality and the dramatic power with which it is conceived. Mr. Wingham provides an instrumental offertory in the shape of an elegant and melodious trio for three solo-violins. The *Sanctus* is written for six-part chorus, and the *Benedictus* is a very beautiful quartett and chorus. The *Agnus Dei* is full of reminiscences of the *Kyrie* although not a repetition. This Mass can be most heartily recommended to our choirs who are on the look out for a good, noble specimen of modern Church Music. Among Mr. Wingham's church compositions he has written a short *Mass in G* (MS.) for three male voices unaccompanied; this would be a boon for our choirs in Lent and Advent if published; another *Mass in G* for four male voices, likewise in MS.; and a fourth *Mass in F* for S.A.T.B. for voices and organ, also unpublished. Two motetts written for Antwerp in honour of St. Joseph: (1.) *Te Joseph*. (2.) *Coelitum Joseph* for voices and orchestra—*Amavit Sapientiam* for unaccompanied voices, quartett with a brilliant concluding chorus, *Confirma hoc, Dextra Domini* and some other pieces for

Holy Week, all of which are still, we regret to say, in MS. A magnificent *Te Deum* for voices and orchestra written for the opening of the new Church of the London Oratory is as fine a piece of Church Music as we can boast of, and if Mr. Wingham can only be persuaded to publish it he will be just supplying a want which the approaching jubilee celebrations have created.

Of Mr. John Francis Barnett, who is so well esteemed for his sound and fine compositions, we cannot say much as regards Church Music, for at present he has published little for the Church. Some motetts and a fine eight-part *Tantum Ergo* make us hope that he will give us many more, and it is with a peculiar pleasure that we hear that he is engaged in writing a Mass which we are sure will be both worthy of its high end and of its composer's reputation.

Mr. F. Westlake has produced a Mass written some years back for voices in unison, and now arranged for four voices. It has met with the greatest approval, and is justly esteemed as being a musicianly creation, and one that will be of much use to our choirs.

Mr. J. Short, a Birmingham musician, has written two Masses which, without coming up to the high standard for instance of Mr. Wingham's work, yet are good and useful productions, and are, we hear, popular with choirs of moderate capabilities.

With the exception of Gounod, who surpasses all his contemporaries in all countries, there seem to be in France no church musicians of note at the present time. Masses and Motetts are produced in abundance, more to the advantage of the printers than to the Art or to the Church, and we cannot recall to mind any names of importance, and this, as we have hinted before, is due to the blighting effects of a constant use of nothing but Plain

Chant. In Belgium there is a more healthy spirit, and the name of Benoit, who has written some charming Church music, is worthy of record. In Germany the efforts of Church Musicians are confined to the narrow groove of the Cecilian Society. The Bohemian composer, Dvorak, has written a wonderful *Stabat Mater*, which never fails to create a profound impression. In Italy music has not made the advance it has in other countries. The nature and character of the people need a different style to what we do in the northern parts of Europe. With Rossi, Cappocci, and Mustapha we have well-nigh exhausted the names of church composers who are known beyond the limits of their own country. Most of the modern Church Music in Italy is in MS., and it is very difficult to obtain copies.

On the whole it seems to me, with the exception of Gounod, that the modern school of Church Music is most worthily represented by England, and perhaps it is only fair; for after the blighting influence of the revolt against the Church, and the days of persecution are over, after "the winter is gone" then "the *flowers* appear in our land." If our musicians receive that support to which they can lay a rightful claim, there is no reason why in England we should not have a school of church composers who will follow the great traditions of the past, and put into modern language the expression of the feelings of true Catholic hearts.

CHAPTER X.

THE USE OF THE ORGAN AND ORCHESTRA IN DIVINE WORSHIP.

A HISTORY of Sacred Music would be incomplete without a notice of the use of instrumental music, for its influence has been immense and has largely helped to build up the musical art of the present day, so I purpose in this chapter to treat of the Organ and Orchestra. Passing by the early history of the stately instrument which from its excellencies is called *the* instrument, it will suffice to say that most probably the first idea of a wind-instrument was suggested by the passing breezes striking against the open ends of broken reeds, and investigation showed that according to the different lengths of the reed, so the pitch of the murmurs varied. Thus it came to pass that a graduated series of reeds were formed into an instrument rough and rude indeed, and were brought under the control of the human breath, and so we had the Pandean pipes or "mouth-organ"; the first step towards that marvellous instrument which adds so much to the solemnity and dignity of Divine worship.

We will now, however, leave the early origin of the organ, tempting subject though it be, and look into its connection with Christian worship. Julianus, a Spanish bishop, in the year 450, speaks of it as being at that time in common use in his country. "In the most ancient city of Grado," an organ is mentioned as belonging to a conventual church before the year 580. The description is left to us, and is interesting. It was two feet long, six inches broad, and furnished fifteen playing-slides (notes), and it had thirty pipes, being two pipes to each note. But it was in 666 that Pope Vitalian introduced it into the Roman churches, and its use then soon became general. According to William of Malmsbury the Saxons had organs long before the Conquest, and we find that in the time of Edgar, St. Dunstan made one for his abbey, with pipes of brass. Pepin, the father of Charlemagne, had one presented to him by the Greek Emperor, and Charlemagne had one made after the Greek model for his church at Aix-la-Chapelle. And by the tenth century the use of the organ seems to have been general. In the time of Chaucer it was well known in England. In the tale of the "Cock and Fox" the line occurs—

> "Merrier than the merry organ
> On Masse-days that in the churches go;"

and in the beautiful "Nonne's Tale,"

> "And while that organs maden melody
> To God alone thus in her hert song she."

Though whether St. Cecilia played the organ or not is a doubtful fact. Most likely the word "organ" is to be taken generically as meaning an instrument of music. It means so in the Scripture, and most likely *Cantantibus organis* is truly rendered, "whilst the instruments of music were being played." But this in passing. Once introduced into Divine service the organ has never lost its place in the Church, and it is too valuable a help to devotion to be dispensed with. True it is that an organ has never been allowed in the Sistine Chapel. But no argument can be brought from that. The Sistine is an institution entirely by itself, and is often found the exception to many a rule. It has its own variations of the Plain Chant, its own peculiar ceremonial, and its own traditions which it preserves even against the letter of express legislation.

Now in its relations to the services of the Church the organ can be viewed in two ways; (1) as having a part by itself, or (2) as used as an accompaniment to the voices. The legislation for the use of the organ, as contained in the official sources, are almost *entirely* concerned with the first relation, and so far have nothing to do with the second. This is a point most carefully to be considered and borne in mind, and its importance will hereafter be seen.

The laws of the Church regarding the use of the organ are contained in the "*Cærimoniale Episcoporum*," Book I., Chapter xxviii., and in some decrees of the Sacred Congregation of Rites. Now the custom which existed when the *Cærimoniale* was compiled was for all the singing—Plain Chant, or Figured Music—to be entirely *unaccompanied*. There was no such thing as accompanied music. The organ's work was playing before and after service, filling up the pauses between either the *accentus* of the sacred ministers or the *concentus* of the choir by what are termed to-day interludes or voluntaries, and "supplying" for the singing. This "supplying" takes place, for instance, at Vespers. When the antiphon is repeated, the organ should play a few bars while a singer recites (mind, not sings) the words of the antiphon; or at the hymn the alternate verses should be recited *sub organo*, *i.e.*, the organ meanwhile playing an interlude. At the Mass, the alternate chants of the *Kyrie*, *Gloria*, *Sanctus*, and *Agnus Dei* may be omitted by the singers, and while the organ plays, the words omitted are then recited by one of the singers. The Tract, Sequence, Offertory and Communion may be also

H

said during an organ interlude. The *Deo Gratias* after the *Ite Missa est*, in like manner, may be said *sub organo*, and also the repetition of the Introit. Thus, according to the *Cærimoniale*, the sole use of the organ is, for instrumental music, pure and simple. Such a thing as accompanying the voice was not thought of nor legislated for, and therefore we see how it was that in the time of penance and mourning the sound of the organ was prohibited.

The use of the organ, as understood and recognized by the compilers of the *Cærimoniale*, is very different from the use that obtains at this present day. *Then* the voices sang unaccompanied by any instrumental aid; *now* musical science has advanced, and has taught us the art of combining into one mighty voice of praise both vocal and instrumental music. So it is clear that, unless we use the style of music in vogue at the period of the compilation of the *Cærimoniale*, we are not, in the absence of later legislation bearing upon the altered state of music, bound by these laws. There is, indeed a case in point and one about which a question is often raised, "whether it is lawful in Masses for the Dead to use the organ as an accompaniment for the voices," *i.e.*, not for voluntaries, interludes, or "supplying" but simply to support the voices. The *Cærimoniale* says the organ is not used in Masses for the Dead; but that does not touch the point, for the only one recognized by that book is that of merely *instrumental* music, not the use of the organ as an accompaniment. But, on the other hand, in a commentary on the *Cæremoniale* compiled by Aloysius Proto of Naples, and recently published by Pustet, there is a decree of the S.C.R., which authorizes its use. These are the words of the decree:—
Organi pulsatio sono mæsto et lugubri permitti potest in Missis defunctorum, etsi renuat Ordinarius. Die 31 *Martii*

1629 *Savonen. n.* 807. This may be taken as meaning that even interludes and supplying are allowed; but, I take it, the general interpretation is that it may be used as a support for the voices. Surely that is more reasonable than in churches, where there is only a small or a weak choir, condeming both the performers and hearers to unaccompanied music. Nothing is so beautiful as good unaccompanied singing, and I remember with delight the exquisite treat I had at the Dom at Cologne last summer when I heard a Palestrina Mass sung in great perfection. There, I may mention, the regulations of the *Cærimoniale* as to the use of the organ are carried out to the letter. But we need not go out of our own country to recall the distressing and painful effect of bad unaccompanied singing. They are too frequent in this country, and too well known by my readers who have often suffered like myself. It would in these cases surely be better to have the accompaniment of the organ *sono mæsto et lugubri* to keep the voices in tune, rather than to destroy all chance of devotion in the hearers.

There are two questions which occur, and in which the style of music at present used calls for no change from the written law. They are, whether the organ should be played during the Elevation, and also at the time of Benediction. Certainly in both cases. As to the Elevation the *Cærimoniale* says: "*Pulsatur . . . . . item dum elevatur SS. Sacramentum graviori et dulciori sono,*" and as to Benediction, the *Ritus Servandus* which is of obligation in this country says, "*Dum datur Benedictio possunt organa pulsari suavi ac gravi sonitu, qui sit aptus ad devotionem et venerationem erga SS. Sacramentum conciliandum,*" and this, we may add, is the prevailing practice in Rome.

Now, as to *what* music should be accompanied by the organ. There is a custom existing of accompanying the *accentus*—

for instance the Preface. But I know of no authority, either for or against this practice. In cases where the priest is gifted with a good voice, and the accompanist is skilful, the effect is certainly not unpleasing. Then as to the music of the Palestrina School an accompaniment of any kind whatsoever is simply ruination. This kind of music is *purely* vocal and depends for its effect upon the voices alone. No one with any artistic feeling would for a moment suggest such a thing as an organ accompaniment to Palestrina. Then as to the music of the Modern School. The accompaniment is mostly designed for an orchestra, and if it is reduced for the organ it should be as much as possible a faithful reproduction of the orchestral effects as far as they can be transferred to the key-board. There are comparatively few Masses of merit written for organ accompaniment pure and simple, and it is to be hoped that our composers will not neglect this part of the field of Church Music.

As to Plain Chant, my conviction is that *any* accompaniment simply spoils the beauty and elasticity of the Chant. As Dr. Witt says, "Plain Chant is pure melody, and was invented and composed without harmonic accompaniment... So any harmonic accompaniment to it is an evil.... even if by the first artist in the world, it is the greatest misfortune; in fact, its death." In the first place, it is an anachronism. Then from the heavy and dead tone of the organ, the singers are overweighted and find it impossible to give that lightness and delicacy to the execution of the chant which it essentially demands. Those who have heard the Plain Chant sung by a choir who have been taught on the true principle and accustomed to sing it without the help of the organ will bear me out in what I say, that the organ simply spoils the chant. If accompaniment must be had, that of stringed instruments is far better, and this perhaps from their nearer approach to the sympathetic power of the human voice. So far for the History and use of the Organ in Divine Service. We now come to the other side of the question of instrumental music, namely that of the Orchestra.

If the use of the organ in Divine worship is sanctioned by the force of ages, still more so is the use of the orchestra—that is, other instruments of music besides the organ. Even as early as the time of the Temple, the use of instruments obtained, and that on a scale of great magnificence. According to the Talmud, the choral services were conducted in this fashion : Standing upon the broad step of the stairway which led from the place of the people to the outer court of the priests, were twelve Levites clothed in the dress of their order ; and when the signal had been given by the clashing of cymbals, they began playing their instruments—namely, nine lyres, two harps, and a pair of cymbals, and sang the praises of God. To them were joined other Levites, who played, but did not sing ; whilst young boys of the Levitical race lifted up their innocent voices and added their pure notes to those of their elder brethren. The pauses in the Psalms and the different divisions were marked by blasts of trumpets by priests who stood on either hand of the players on cymbals. Throughout the Psalms, we often have allusions to musical instruments, especially in the last one, a Psalm of rejoicing, which bears signs of having been written for an occasion of public joy. " Praise Him with the sound of *trumpet*, praise Him with *psaltery* (a kind of dulcimer) and *harp*. Praise Him with *timbrel* (a hand-drum) and choir, praise Him with *strings* and *organs* (other instruments). Praise Him on high-sounding *cymbals*." Here is a large orchestra, and it gives us an idea how majestically the services of the Temple were performed.

In Christian times, on the authority of Justin the Martyr and Eusebius, the use of instrumental music, from the earliest days, took its place in the assemblies of the faithful. About this there cannot be much improbability, as it is not unlikely that at the same time that the Church took and made her own the pagan vocal music so also she took up the use of instrumental music, which was connected with that style of singing. Indeed, we find very early in Church History protests from the ultra purists of those days, who clamoured against instrumental music as being pagan and Judaizing. How history repeats itself! A little later on we hear of St. Ambrose introducing instrumental music as a help to the singing of his people; and one is familiar with the constant tradition of St. Cecilia accompanying herself upon musical instruments whilst she sang to her Lord, "Make Thou my heart without stain."

But during the middle ages the musicians gave all their attention to the voices, and but little care was bestowed upon instrumental music; and it was not until the period of the Transition, about which we have written in a former chapter, that instrumental music regained its rightful place as a powerful auxiliary to devotion. That the orchestra can be used in our churches is an undoubted fact, and on feast days there is nothing which adds so much to the outward splendour and majesty of a function as the introduction of an orchestra. Indeed, it places at the hand of the musician a power of expression which is above everything else—a power which is productive of the highest good. All the masterpieces of modern Church Music have been written for an orchestral accompaniment, and demand it for the full expression of the composer's conception. Who has heard sung *Beethoven in C* with simply an organ accompaniment, and then again with the full orchestra? The one bears the same relation to the other as an original oil-painting, glowing in colour, rich, varied and harmonious, and an engraving, in which it is impossible to reproduce all the artist's colour-effects.

Now, what does a Church orchestra consist of, or rather, what instruments are required for a due rendering of the Masses of the Great Masters? As a rule we would require first and second violins, violas, cellos, and double basses; flutes, oboes, clarionettes, bassoons, horns, trumpets, trombones, tympani—*i.e.*, kettledrums, which are not only instruments of percussion, but also sound a real note, and therefore can sustain the harmony. This will afford, as a rule we say, quite sufficient variety to secure the fulfilment of the composer's intention. Indeed, Mozart very frequently wrote for a much smaller orchestra—sometimes only for the strings, and has left us many works in which we marvel at his consummate skill in getting such fine effects out of such slender means. Haydn, again, in the *Sixteenth Mass*, does without flutes, oboes, bassoons, horns, and trombones, but he adds the organ as an *obligato* instrument. In the more modern scores of Beethoven, Schubert, and Cherubini, the above instruments would all be needed.

Now, there is no *direct* legislation on the subject of orchestral instruments, as far as I am aware. There are certain decrees and instructions which are useful as showing the mind of the Church, but which are only of *local* force. The short reference made to instrumental music in the *Cæremoniale* is, as I submit, regarding an entirely different state of affairs than now exists, and therefore is not to the present purpose. But in a recent Instruction issued in 1884 to the Bishops of Italy by the Sacred Congregation of Rites, which I purpose in a future chapter to give *in extenso*, we find "Instruments which are too noisy, such as side and big drums (*N.B. The tympani or kettledrums are not excluded*), cymbals, instruments used by street musicians (*e.g.*, *hurdy-gurdy*, *guitar*, *concertinas*, *castanettes*, &c.), and the pianoforte, &c., are prohibited. Nevertheless trumpets, flutes, kettledrums, and the like which were used by the people of Israel to accompany the praises of God—the Canticles and Psalms of David—are allowed on the condition that they be skilfully used, and only in moderation, especially at the *Tantum Ergo* at Benediction." So, as far as this instruction has force, all the orchestral instruments I have mentioned above are allowed, and may be used, though why cymbals are excluded I do not know, for they were certainly used in the Temple.

There is a little note which is year by year printed in the Ordo for the Three last days of Holy Week and which serves as a witness that the use of the orchestra in church is recognized and allowed. The note says that *musical instruments* are not to be used in any way in the liturgical office of these Three Days. It is clear, therefore, that for the other days in the year they may be used. The late Canon Oakley, in his well thought-out pamphlet, *On Church Music and Church Choirs*, says: "It is, of course, perfectly competent to local Superiors to make such regulations on the subject of Church Music as they may consider expedient; and I think, if I remember right, that Dr. Griffiths, when Vicar-Apostolic of the London district, made certain laws in this department of his administration which were abrogated by his large-minded and accomplished successor."

The question of orchestral accompaniments is bound up with the use of Modern Music, and, if one is condemned, away must go the other. We cannot consistently admit the Art creations of these days without taking them as a whole. That the Church uses all the various kinds of music, and has made none of them (with the exception of the Plain Chant for the *accentus*) more her own than another is a fact which I have endeavoured to make clear in these pages, and therefore the style which needs orchestral accompaniments, as an integral part of the design, is as much in place in the Divine Service as the Plain Chant or Palestrina. As regards the question of taste and expediency, there are some peculiar souls who delight in nothing but archaic music (musical fossils, one might call them), others who prefer *no* music at all during Mass; but the greater majority of the Faithful, the *sanior pars*, delight in it, and find it a great help in their devotion. And as to expediency, of course I am supposing that the accompaniment is well done, otherwise it is a distraction instead of a help to devotion. There is another object attained by the use of the orchestra in church which I will only just mention. It is this: many amateur musicians are thereby induced to devote their abilities to the service of the Church. There is scope in our churches not only for those gifted with the finest musical instrument in existence —the singing voice—but also for those who are not gifted in that manner, but who have the power of performing upon orchestral instruments. "Let *every* spirit praise the Lord," not only "in choirs," but also "in strings and other musical instruments." The Church approves by her legislation, and encourages the practice by her use, therefore let no one condemn.

NOTE.—An esteemed correspondent has called my attention to the *typical* edition of the *Cærimoniale* brought out last year at Ratisbon. *A propos* of the use of the organ in Requiems, the *Cærimoniale* now says:—"In the Office for the Dead the organ is not used; but in the Masses, if music is used, the organ is silent, when the singing ceases. This also can be used in Advent and on the Serial days of Lent." This establishes the point that the organ can be used as an *accompaniment* in Masses for the dead.

CHAPTER XI.

ON THE PRESENT STATE OF CHURCH MUSIC IN THIS COUNTRY.

WE have discussed the growth of Church Music from its earliest stages until its perfect development in the works of the masters of these later days. It will not be without interest to my readers, I hope, if we take a more particular look at the present state of Church Music in this country, and examine its prospects and needs. And here I may remark that in England we are peculiarly fortunate in our position as regards Church Music. We are bound by no fetters of the tradition of years—a slavery which often clogs and deadens all spirit of progress, and which serves as an excuse for self-satisfied sleepiness. We are free to choose and combine all the glorious work of the past with all the wonderful creations of modern genius, and so we are able to select the best works of musical genius of all styles and use them to the glory and honour of Him Who inspired them. Our subject, then, naturally divides itself into two heads—(*a*) our music, and (*b*) our choirs.

From time to time there crops up in the Catholic Press a controversy about Church Music. It seems to be a chronic epidemic. Many letters are written; generally, however, on any other point than the one in question. Much ink and paper are used. Decrees of the S. C. R.

are thrown about in a perfectly reckless manner, without regard to their meaning or applicability. Sarcasm, not unmixed with a certain spice of personality, is abundant, and with what result? That we all go on as merrily as before, and, to paraphrase some well-known lines,—

> But what gives rise to no little surprise,
> Nobody seems one penny the worse.

Now, if I may venture to class the various writers who take part in these periodical encounters, I take them as representing the three schools of Church Music. There is the Plain Chantist—a kind of rabid musical teetotaler of the most advanced school. Nothing but Plain Chant will satisfy him. With that we do not quarrel. Tastes are various; but the worst is he does not want us to be satisfied with anything else. He wants to rob us of the liberty we enjoy in the Church of God and bind us down into one narrow groove, according to the dictates of his own sweet fancy. "My worthy good friend," we may say to him, "it gives us a peculiar thrill of pleasure to know that your devotion and religious sentiments are stirred up by Plain Chant. We respect you, nay, we look upon you with a certain amount of awe, as being a peculiar being, different from the rest of mankind. But permit us to say, with all due deference to your many excellent qualities, that *we* are not constituted upon the same noble model as you are. Plain Chant, far from filling us with devotion, depresses us. The truth is we do not understand it; it is a language which does not convey to our souls anything intelligible. Had we lived in the thirteenth century we should no doubt have understood it; but it is our misfortune—not our fault, we assure you—to be living in the nineteenth century. Plain Chant is no more intelligible to us now-a-days than you would be if you were to get up into one of our pulpits and discourse to us in Chaucerian English." I have put in this fashion the general feeling there is about Plain Chant and its *exclusive* use. Music is for the people, not the people for the music, and although I, personally—if I may venture to bring myself into the matter—admire greatly and take a delight in joining to the best of my poor abilities in the Plain Chant, yet I am convinced it does not do for our people. It does not appeal to them, it does not awake in them any echoes of the religious life. The impressions it produces are gloom and monotony, and these are not religious. One explanation may be that Plain Chant essentially demands a knowledge of Latin, both on the part of the singer and on the part of the hearer. And where this knowledge is wanting the Chant is lifeless and without character or meaning. Who will assert that this knowledge is not wanting both in our average choristers and our congregations? The truth is that Plain Chant is suited to and can only be sung, as it ought to be sung, by the clergy and religious. With them it is safe; with others it is a dangerous weapon of offence. The attitude of the laity towards Plain Chant is illustrated by the following story:—A very ardent admirer of the Chant was once talking to a lady—who, by the bye, is not wholly unknown to me—about his hobby. She informed him that she found she always prayed better in a church where nothing but Plain Chant was used. Greatly delighted was the gentleman, and he proceeded to explain how one mode produced sentiments of joy, another of grief, when she stopped him by saying, "I always pray better because I am obliged to shut my ears so as not to listen to the 'row.'"

There is then the advocate of Plain Chant who condescends to human infirmity so far as to allow figured music in the Palestrina style, yet in whose nostrils Mozart and Haydn savour as an abomination. Our second friend is as unreasonable as the rabid musical teetotaler who forswears all save Plain Chant, and for precisely the same reason. And to his unreasonableness he adds inconsistency; for he does not see that Mozart and Haydn are simply natural developments of the reforms which the great Palestrina introduced. He it was who introduced, or at least firmly fixed, the dramatic principle in his works, and who filled his compositions with that very same spirit which we find, with due regard to growth, in the works of the modern school. Now, practically, the people do not understand Palestrina's musical works. To a musician they will always be a delight and a pleasure, but they are caviare to the generality of people. A case in point. Some years ago, when I was directing the music at a West-end church, I arranged for the patronal festival a performance of Palestrina's *Missa Papæ Marcelli*. Added to the ordinary choir of the church were some picked voices from all the best London choirs. Unusual pains and care were taken so as to insure a good performance, and with what result? The musicians who were present—and they were numerous, for the service had been announced in the daily press—were delighted both with the work and, they were kind enough to say, with the manner in which it was rendered. And the people?—they cared nothing at all about it. They neither understood nor appreciated it. In fact I had many requests not to give them any more of it!

Cardinal Bartolini, the Prefect of the S. C. R., says in a famous letter of his, which fell rather like a bomb-shell among the advocates of nothing but Plain Chant or Palestrina—

"The Italian ear (*and if Italian how much more the English?*), too much accustomed to the sounds of the organ, feels no pleasure in the beautiful harmonies of Palestrina. . . . Whilst to the true lover of music the effect is wonderful, the ordinary run of hearers, unacquainted with the art, think that these beautiful compositions—echoes of the melodies of Paradise—are only a confusion of voices. Hence, if Palestrina's music were much used, there would be a danger that the faithful, generally unable to appreciate what is sublime, would not attend services where music was used which would not be fortunate enough to please them." This just hits the right nail on the head, and I commend it to the consideration of my readers, not only for what it says about Palestrina, but also as enunciating the principle that music is for the people, and that those concerned with the music in our churches should take care to provide the people with such music as they can appreciate.

Now there is a third class of correspondents who enter eagerly into musical controversy, and they are just as unreasonable and inconsistent as the other two classes—I mean those who would exclude Plain Chant and Palestrina and leave nothing but the modern school. I have endeavoured to lay down the principle that the Church uses all three kinds of music—all have a place in her services—all are good in their degree—all are of use. It is, therefore, a mistake to exclude any style, and a choir properly constituted should be proficient in all the styles and use them all. In the 'lists, which I give at the end of this history, of Masses which should find a place in all our choirs, it will be seen that all the various styles of music are represented, and a place is found for each. About the modern school I may add that, in the letter above mentioned, Cardinal Bartolini says, "The compositions of Haydn, and the Masses of Mozart, of Cherubini, and of others, are choice and serious compositions, and are far from being unbecoming the holiness of the Church." This will be a crumb of comfort to the advocates of the modern school when they are attacked by the acrimonious diatribes of their opponents.

Here, under a description of the three classes of writers on musical controversy, I have given my views, for what they are worth, upon the present state of music. I suppose until the end of the chapter such controversies will go on, for there will be extreme partisans in each school. But I have endeavoured to show the weak point in all their arguments and positions, in the hope that it will be seen that the best thing to do is to preserve all that is good and to use it; thus imitating, as I have said before, the Prudent Householder bringing "out of his treasures things new and old." If this little history proves a kind of olive branch, and contributes in any way towards a peaceful understanding, on the principle of "live and let live," it won't be without its use.

The second division of our subject takes up the question of our choirs :—

In treating, then, of our choirs I will make a threefold division. There is the choir attached to our large churches, which is, or ought to be, highly trained and capable of performing the highest class music of every school. Then, in our smaller town and provincial churches, there is the choir composed mostly of amateurs, who too frequently *think* themselves capable of singing the works of the great masters. The third class to be considered is that of the small country missions, who suffer from two things—the difficulty of getting any singers, and of getting any music at all. Now, to proceed in scholastic fashion, each of these divisions of choirs may be again subdivided into other three classes, according to their constitution. Thus, a choir consists of boys and men, of men only, or of women and men. We will take this last division first, and now discuss the constitution of our choirs.

After twelve years of practical experience I am fully convinced that boys are quite capable of executing all Church Music, that is all music which is good art, and is worthy of the name of Church Music. There is something so simple and innocent about 'a boy's voice which gives to it a charm which is found in no other kind of voice. There is an absence of that exaggerated sentiment which so many of our adult singers delight in, and which often serves as a means of disguising their poverty of tone, and in its place we have in the boy that natural expression which is so suited to Church Music. Indeed we may say, in passing, that often the charge of " staginess," which is sometimes brought against modern Church Music, is due, with whatever truth there may be in the charge, to the false and exaggerated interpretation given to the work, and not to the work itself. Of course there are boys and boys, but I do contend that, with patience and skill on the part of the choirmaster, almost all boys can be taught to sing and to use their voices in the proper manner. Our best boy singers come from the middle class, and this can be accounted for by the home surroundings, which have a refining influence upon the child, whereas in the poor classes that refinement is wanting; and although they can be trained, yet they take more care and trouble than perhaps the choirmaster, unless very devoted, cares to give. There is just this difference : the poor boy is accustomed to play in the streets and to shout, and in this shouting he always uses his chest-notes. When he comes to sing, he sings in the same manner, with fearful energy, right up the scale as far as he can go at the top of his voice, in a coarse and grating tone, naturally out of tune, and then breaks. Whereas the boy whose home-surroundings are more refined is not accustomed to use that same harsh tone, *i.e.*, his chest-notes, and when he comes to sing, naturally falls into using his head-notes, and sings with the same tone of voice that he would plead with his mother. It is in the correct use of the two registers of the singing voice (the so-called chest-notes and the head-notes) that the difference lies between the trained boy's voice—clear and round in tone like a flute—and that of the untrained boy, whose musical performance can only be likened to the war-whoops of wild Indians or the fearful tones of a fog-horn! Wherever there is a school attached to a mission there boys can be found. It is not the lack of boys which creates the difficulty, but the lack of choirmasters. That is the obstacle, and not until we have choirmasters who make a special subject of training boys shall we be in a better state. I am speaking of good chorus boys, who, I contend, are always to be had. Of course, boys with exceptional voices, capable of singing the highest class music, are not always easily found, and when found are generally snapped up by the larger churches. One need not say that a choir of boys and men is more in accordance with the mind of the Church, and is *the* state to be aimed at. A question connected with this one of the boys is whether they should be used for singing alto or second treble part, or whether the adult alto should be used. The last-named is a necessary evil, I fear, at present; though, when boys can be had to sing the alto part, there can be no doubt of the advantage in the increased richness and tone. The adult alto, unless his voice is remarkably good, is a distressing creature, and causes much trouble to the choirmaster and infliction to the congregations.

As to choirs consisting only of men, I think that they are often resorted to as being easier to keep together than if boys were used. Undoubtedly, this is so, for the adult male singer, as a rule, knows how to sing, and does not require to be trained in the same measure as the boy. But is the result

I

as pleasing? To me—and I think that I am in accord with the general opinion—a Mass sung entirely by tenors and basses is very heavy and depressing. And then, from the limited *répertoire* of Masses for tenors and basses, a choirmaster is under the temptation of perpetrating such musical atrocities as the following. In a well-known West-end church which is much frequented, and where they are supposed to have "such lovely music" (wild horses will not drag from me the precise locality), a choir of tenors and basses *calmly* sang in my own hearing, and to my great disgust, Gounod's beautiful *Messe Solennelle de Ste. Cecile.* The way the work of the unfortunate composer was hacked and cut about was simply scandalous. The vocal parts were inverted, and the result was discreditable to any one with the slightest artistic feeling.

Regarding mixed choirs of men and women, little need be said. Their use was a matter of temporary convenience, and by the Provincial Councils of Westminster they are condemned, and it is ordered that, as soon as possible, male choirs be substituted. This order was enforced in the Archdiocese of Westminster about twenty years ago by the present Cardinal Archbishop; but as yet the other Bishops of England have not, as far as I know, deemed it expedient to enforce it throughout their dioceses. Still it has to be aimed at, and it is "a consummation most devoutly to be wished for." To some people the voice of a woman in church is absolutely repugnant, and I must confess that I am among the number who feel thus. *Mulier tacet in Ecclesia* is a blessed saying, and "worthy of all acceptance." But as this is dangerous ground I am treading on with my fair readers, I will say no more but take up my position under the shield of authority and æsthetic requirements!

Having disposed of our choirs regarding their constitution, I fall back upon my first division, and consider them as regards the music they should sing. Now, first of all, I would make the basis of every choir the *Graduale Romanum*; not only the music for the changeable parts of the Mass, but also for the ordinary. This, mind, for all choirs, little or great, simple or highly trained. This point being secured, I would point out that in the choirs attached to the large churches, and consisting mostly of professional artists, they should not confine themselves to any one school. One gets tired of a perpetual course of Haydn and Mozart. They are admirable for the greater festivals of the year, but seem, with the exception of the smaller Masses (alas! too little heard), out of place on the ordinary Sunday. It is like, pardon the simile, having plum-pudding *all* the year round! Our first-class choirs are too exclusive and too conservative, and it is wonderful what a limited stock of Masses they have. They want more "go" and energy. It is, of course, more trouble to get up new work than to keep up the old, and then there is a natural antipathy against rehearsals on the part of the singers. The result of this is often that not only is no new music learnt, but the old stock Masses are sung, in a slip-shod and careless fashion, which is very discreditable. No music ought to be sung at Mass without having been previously carefully rehearsed. I don't believe in "music we know well enough"; that generally means "music with the same old mistakes." Another effect this exclusiveness has is that living composers have no encouragement to devote their talents to Church Music, and so the art in this particular department is brought to a standstill. When shall we hear of our larger churches emulating the example of Antwerp, and offering a prize for the best Mass? I fear that our clergy at present are not alive to the important influence of Church Music, and give but little encouragement to it.

Of the smaller churches in town and country, the prevailing sin is ambition. Some member of the choir hears at a larger church—say, one of Haydn's Masses. He or she (generally *she*) is at once seized with the spirit of emulation. "We must *do* that at our church." Now, the spirit of emulation is good when it succeeds; if it does not, Pride has a fall, and the worst is that Church Music suffers. It is the incompetent and ambitious attempt of small choirs to perform music which is far above them that brings such discredit upon Church Music, and gives the enemy cause to blaspheme. I once heard somewhere in the South of England a choir, consisting of three women (two who were uncertain both in age and voice) and two men, getting through Haydn No. 1. It was something awful; and when I just mention the fact that the organist only played from "ear," it may be imagined what was the result. I was told beforehand that the choir was considered particularly good. The music they attempted undoubtedly is so, but the execution——poor Haydn!

I have spoken thus hardly, perhaps, on the smaller choirs, and reverence to the beauty of holiness demands it; but I will now say that it is not entirely their own fault. I look upon it, in a measure, as being the expression of a want which is greatly felt, and in no place more than in the small choir. It is this. We have no good, short, and easy Masses. The feebleness and mild inanities of Webbe, Ett, Concone, Bordese, *et hoc genus omne*, are painful in the extreme, and it is, perhaps, in utter disgust with these productions that our small choirs attempt the greater things with disastrous results. I said above, "We have no good, short, and easy Masses." I ought to have said, "we *had*," for I am glad to say that there is at last a movement in the right direction. Mr. Alphonse Cary is publishing *The Catholic Chorister*, a collection of easy music for small choirs. One piece is a *Mass in A^b*, by Mr. A. E. Tozer, a remarkably well-written and musicianly Mass. Mr. Tozer's taste and capabilities are of a high order, and it was therefore with a peculiar pleasure that I heard that he is engaged upon a second Mass. The *Mass in A^b* is worthy of the attention of all choirs, both simple and high class. A *Mass in E^b*, by Mr. C. Forrester, F.C.O., is well written and pleasing, and is sure to be a favourite, while in a *Mass in D* Mr. Cary shows us that he, also, can write good easy music. Will not our other English musicians come to the help of our small choirs? There is a large field for them. There is no reason why short easy music should be inane and mediocre, and that is the danger which one who seeks to provide easy music for small choirs is particularly liable to fall into. If Mr. Cary will give us more music of the standard of excellence to which Mr. Tozer's music attains, he will be sure of getting support, and well-known men or new composers of merit can be got to do the work, but the feeble productions of half-fledged students of harmony ought carefully to be avoided. The claims also of the very small country choirs ought to be kept in view, and their wants supplied with Masses in unison or two parts. I just throw out a suggestion to our composers whether they could not utilize more the *chant-form* for simple unison Masses. We have the precedent for it in the Plain-Chant Masses, and I think it might be usefully applied to easy Masses of the modern school.

To sum up, I look upon the present state of Church Music in England as hopeful, and as certainly in an enviable position of freedom. Our principal wants are capable choirmasters, and good easy music for smaller choirs. With the advance which music is making among all classes these two wants will be remedied, and as a means towards attaining these ends I throw out the suggestion that something might be done by the formation of Diocesan Choral Associations. I will not enter upon this subject now, though perhaps at some future time I may do so, but I meanwhile commend the suggestion to the attention of those interested in the subject of Church Music.

CHAPTER XII.

CONCLUSION.

IN bringing this History of Church Music to a conclusion, after having traced its growth from the earliest times till these present days, I do not think that I can do better than reproduce some instructions which were sent in 1884 to the Bishops of Italy on the subject of Church Music. As they are, I believe, the latest instructions on the subject, they will be not only of interest but of use as an extra proof of the truth I have been endeavouring to maintain—viz., that the Church gives us the greatest latitude in the matter of the Music of the Sanctuary, and considers nothing as unworthy of the Service of God that is good art. All that are good, beautiful, and true, bear upon their face the impress of Him Whose Goodness, Beauty, and Truth they reflect; and, therefore, they are not unworthy as an offering to His Majesty. These instructions are, of course, of only local force, but yet contain so strong an evidence of the Church's mind that they are most valuable—and are, besides, so admirable that they might well serve as a model for similar diocesan purposes. It may be well to remark that they are directed to Italian bishops. Now in Italy, Church Music is in a very different state to what it is in other countries. The national characteristics of the people demand a style of music which to us Northerners of a less ardent disposition appears frivolous, light, and perhaps undignified. Again, on the other hand, Mozart and Haydn's music have made no way in Italy, and why? Because they are *too* solemn and dry for the Italian ear. They are in *stile tedesco*, which is synonymous according to their ideas with all that is dry, dull, and uninteresting. So it is only fair for us to judge of Italian music from their point of view. If we don't like it we are not obliged to use it; but if it fulfils its purpose in those for whom it was written, *ne impedias musicam*. I, then, here reproduce the instructions, attaching to each section some words of comment.

REGULATIONS FOR SACRED MUSIC.

General rules as to "figured" sacred music, vocal and instrumental, which is authorised or forbidden by the Church.

1. The "figured" vocal music which is authorised by the Church is that only whose grave and pious strains are suited to the house of the Lord, to the Divine praises, and which, by following the meaning of the Sacred Word, help to excite the faithful to devotion. The composition of vocal music in the figured form shall be regulated according to these principles, even when accompanied by the organ and other instruments.

2. The figured music for the organ must answer to the *legato*, harmonious and grave character of this instrument. Instrumental accompaniments in general ought to give a support to the voice, and not overpower it with its loudness. The interludes on the organ or by the orchestra, being original, should always correspond with the solemn tone of the sacred Liturgy.

3. The language proper to the Church being Latin, that language should alone be employed in the composition of figured sacred music. Motetts shall be taken from the Scriptures, the Breviary, the Roman Missal, the Hymns of St. Thomas Aquinas, or of some other Doctor of the Church, or from any other hymns approved and used by the Church.

4. The vocal and instrumental music which is forbidden

by the Church is that which by its character or by the form which it takes tends to distract the faithful in the house of prayer.

In the 1st paragraph quoted we have clearly expressed the dramatic principle which animated Palestrina and his successors in the Modern School. The music should "follow the meaning of the Sacred Words" and so "help to excite the faithful to devotion." Colourless settings of the text are not to be desired or used. Let the joy of the *Gloria* be clearly expressed—the tenderness of the *Agnus Dei* be clearly brought out, and so on. Not only let the meaning of the words be expressed, but also the spirit of the Festival. Thus a more hopeful and even joyous strain is not out of place in the *Kyrie* on Easter Sunday, for the spirit of the day demands it.

The 2nd paragraph contains an artistic regulation as regards accompaniments, and in this as throughout one recognizes the Church as the true Mistress of Art.

Paragraph 4, read together with the first one, seems to imply that the faithful are distracted by music which does not appeal to them.

Special Prohibitions concerning Vocal Music in Church.

5. All kinds of vocal music composed upon *theatrical or profane themes or selections, are expressly forbidden in church*; as well as music of too light or too sensuous a style, such as *cabaletta* or *cavatina*, or recitatives of a theatrical nature. Solos, duetts and trios are permitted, provided they have the character of sacred music, and are part of the consecutive whole of the composition.

6. All music is forbidden in which the words of the Sacred Text are omitted, even to the smallest extent, or transposed, cut up, *too often* repeated, or only intelligible with difficulty.

7. It is forbidden to divide into *over-detached* portions the phrases of the sacred text in the *Kyrie, Gloria, Credo,*

&c., at the expense of the unity of the whole; and also to hurry the singing at certain parts of the Office, such as the responses to the celebrant, the *Introit, Sequence, Sanctus, Benedictus,* the *Agnus Dei,* in the Mass; the *Psalms, Antiphons, Hymn* and *Magnificat* at Vespers. The omission, however, of the *Gradual, Tract, Offertory,* and *Communion,* is allowed under some special circumstances, *e.g.*, want of voices, if the organ supply the deficiency.

8. A disorderly mixture of figured music and plain chant is forbidden; hence it is forbidden to make what are called musical *points* in the *Passion,* in which the Chant given in the *Directorum chori* must be scrupulously adhered to. The sole exception is with regard to the responses of the *Turba* in polyphonal music, which may be sung after the fashion of the Roman school, especially Palestrina.

9. All singing is forbidden which would prolong the Divine offices beyond the prescribed limits of noon in the case of Mass, and of the Angelus in that of Vespers and Benediction, except in those churches where there are privileges or tolerated customs, in which the offices may extend beyond these limits subject to the decision of the Ordinary.

10. It is forbidden to make use of over-affected inflections of the voice, to make too much noise in beating time and giving orders to the performers, to turn one's back on the altar, to chatter, or to do anything else whatever which is out of place in the holy place. It is to be desired that the choir-loft should not be over the main entrance of the church, and that the performers should, as far as possible, be unseen, subject to the prudent regulation of the Ordinary.

The 5th paragraph forbids all adaptations from theatrical sources. This all true Church musicians will most heartily endorse. There is nothing so pernicious, and which strikes more at the root of Church Music than a practice which sometimes exists of adapting Sacred Words to some favourite air out of an opera. I have heard Gounod's lovely *Quando a te lieta* from *Faust* sung as an *O Salutaris*. To put it at the lowest it is bad art, and is irreverent both to the majesty of Divine Service and (though, of course, only in an artistic sense) to the genius of the musician, who deserves at least that his art creations should be treated with respect. I repeat here what I have said elsewhere. The Church has no need to descend to the theatre for her music. She has too many treasures of her own to stand in need of any meretricious adaptions from secular sources. It will be well to note that the idea that *Solos*, &c., are forbidden is entirely erroneous.

The 4th paragraph calls for consideration, as it bears on the question of the omission of words and repetitions. Two things are clear. No words are to be omitted, and repetitions are not forbidden. Now, as regards the omission of the words, I have referred to the fact that in some of Mozart's and Haydn's Masses some portions of the Sacred Text have been omitted by the composers. I am not concerned here with defending such omissions, but I contend that in most cases the words can be supplied by any choirmaster of average ability. But in the cases (and they are *very few*) where the music will not allow of the addition, what is to be done? Can we not do the same as we are undoubtedly allowed to do with the Plain Chant, excepting the *Credo*, for which there is special legislation? I mean for one singer to *recite* the words which are left out. This seems to get over the difficulty. In a description of this practice of "supplying," I would refer my reader to Chapter X., in which I treat of the use of the organ as laid down in the *Cærimoniale Episcoporum*. But in certain cases some of the words *have* to be omitted, *e.g.*, in the *Sanctus*, so that the celebrant should not be kept waiting. This shows that the singing of *every* word is not essential. For instance, in Palestrina's *Missa Papæ Marcelli*, it is necessary to leave out the *Hosanna* in the *Sanctus*, otherwise it would be too long; and this, I understand, is invariably done in Rome itself whenever this masterpiece is performed. Concerning repetitions, they are certainly allowed whenever the due working out of the musical design requires them. Of course, repetition for repetition's sake is bad art, and so is any excess, and therefore it is rightly prohibited. But such repetition is not found in the works of the great masters. They had a definite musical design, and when they repeated a word or a phrase it was an integral portion of their plan, and so was not *too often* repeated. If repetitions *per se* are to be condemned, Palestrina must go, for, to take an example, in the *Missa Papæ Marcelli* he frequently repeats the *Kyrie, Sanctus, Hosanna, Miserere*, &c. Repetitions of the words are not so objectionable as repetition of notes to a syllable. In some of the old Plain Chant Masses one finds sometimes 200 notes to one syllable! This latter seems to me to make the words "intelligible only with difficulty."

In paragraph 7 we note that it is lawful to omit the singing of the *Gradual Tract, Offertory*, and *Communion*.

Paragraph 9 refers to the custom abroad of having the High Mass at an earlier hour than we are in the habit of having it. Our hour is generally eleven. The Liturgical hour is after Terce—*i.e.*, about nine o'clock. This regulation, then, gives three hours as a limit for a High Mass! That is a wide enough margin, in all conscience.

Paragraph 10 should be commended to the attention of the members of our choirs. A well-known American writer, speaking of the usual bad behaviour of a choir, says (I am quoting from memory): "I once heard of a church choir that was not ill-behaved. I forget the name of the place. All that I remember is that it was a very long time ago."

Special prohibitions with regard to Instrumental Music in Church and Composition.

11. It is stringently forbidden to play in church even the minutest portion of theatrical or operatic selections; or of any dance music such as *polkas, waltzes, mazurkas, minuets, rondos, schottisches, varsoviennes, quadrilles, contredanses, polonaises*, &c., and of profane pieces, *e.g., national hymns, popular songs, love and comic songs, ballads*, &c.

12. Instruments which are too noisy are prohibited, such as side and big drums, cymbals, &c., instruments used by street musicians, and the pianoforte. Nevertheless, trumpets, flutes, kettle-drums and the like—which were used among the people of Israel to accompany the praises of God, the Canticles and Psalms of David—are allowed—on the condition that they be skilfully and in moderation used—especially during the *Tantum ergo* at Benediction.

13. Improvisation of *Voluntaries* on the organ is forbidden to those who cannot do it fittingly, *i.e.*, in a manner which respects, not only the rules of art, but the piety and recollection of the faithful.

14. In composition, the following rules must be observed:—The *Gloria* must not be divided into too many detached portions with theatrical solos thrown in between. The *Credo* must also be composed as a consecutive whole, and if it is divided into concerted pieces, these must be so disposed as to form one well connected whole. Solos and duets, after the manner of theatrical compositions with very high notes (not to call them shrieks) for the voice should be avoided as much as possible; for they distract the devotion of the faithful. And above all, care must be taken that the words occupy the exact place they have in the text and not be inverted.

Paragraph 11 calls for little comment. No church musician would tolerate anything approaching such abuses.

In the chapter "on the use of the orchestra" (X.) we have discussed at length paragraph 12, and we have seen that all instruments required for the complete rendering of the orchestral Masses of the great masters are allowed.

Who has not heard the unhappy wanderings over the organ keys of the incompetent musician when he attempts to improvise; and who has not longed for some such regulation as contained in paragraph 13 to be enforced?

Paragraph 14 calls for no comment. It is simply the expression of the principles which have ever guided the great artists.

Paragraphs 15, 16, 17, and 20 relate to the choice of books, and recommend certain Italian publications, "not as of obligation to the exclusion of others that may be arranged or published by other editors, with the approval of their respective Ordinaries according to the rules of the present Instructions," and provides that the parish priests should see to the due carrying out of these orders.

18. The performance of pieces only, published or unpublished, will be allowed in church, which are catalogued in the *Diocesan Index of Repertoires*, and which bear the countersign, stamp, and *visa* of the *Commission of St. Cecilia* and of its Inspector-President, who—in union with the Commission, and always under the immediate jurisdiction of the Ordinary, without prejudice to the authority of local superiors—may even supervise the performance on the spot, request to inspect the music already or about to be performed, and examine into the matter of their compliance with the regulations and with the papers authenticated by the countersign, stamp, and *visa*. He may also report to the Ordinary, and obtain the application of energetic measures against those who transgress.

19. Organists and choir-masters will devote all their efforts and their talent to the best possible execution of the music catalogued in that repertory. They may also employ their science in the enriching it with new compositions, provided these are in conformity with the aforesaid regulations, from which no one can be dispensed. Even the members of the Commission shall be subject to the revision of their work by their fellow members.

21. The above-named Commissions shall be formed of ecclesiastics, and also of laymen skilled in musical science

and animated by a true Catholic spirit. The Diocesan Inspector must be always an ecclesiastic. The nomination and appointment of each and all appertains by right to the Ordinary.

22. To prepare a better future for sacred music in Italy, it is desirable that the Ordinaries should take steps to found schools for teaching figured music on the most perfect and best authorized methods, or to improve those already existing in the ecclesiastical institutions of their respective dioceses, especially in the seminaries. To this end it would be advisable also to open special schools for sacred music in the principal centres of the Peninsula, in order to train up good singers, organists, and choir-masters, as has already been done so laudably in Milan.

23. These regulations shall be forwarded to all the Most Reverend Bishops, who will communicate them to the clergy, organists, and choir-masters of their respective dioceses, and shall be in force in *one month* after such communication by the Ordinary. These regulations, moreover, shall be affixed to a board in the church, placed near the organist's seat, so that they may not on any excuse be transgressed.

It will be well to understand in connection with paragraphs 15 and 16, and the others in this section, that the Society of St. Cecilia referred to is not identical with the German Cecilian Society. It is one which has in view the restoring of the true artistic style of Church Music in Italy in place of the many abuses, as are hinted at in paragraph 11, which unhappily exist.

The remaining paragraphs refer to an admirable project, which, if carried out in the wide and Catholic spirit of these Instructions, would do much good. The danger of such a Commission would be lest it should be in the hands of a narrow-minded *clique*, who, possessed with some unhappy hobby, would endeavour to force it upon all others. But this, with the characteristic wisdom of Rome, is prevented by paragraph 21, which provides that besides ecclesiastics, "laymen who are skilled in musical science and animated by a true Catholic spirit," should be included in the Commission. This would exclude the well-meaning but dangerous officiousness of incompetent amateurs, who are not "skilled in musical science," and also of that other class who are not "animated with a true Catholic spirit." Nothing would give me greater pleasure than to see such a Commission formed among us, for I am sure it will be of the greatest use both to the Church and to that Art which has grown up in the bosom of the Church.

In these pages I have endeavoured to "*praise men of renown . . . . such as by their skill sought out musical tunes, and published canticles of the Scriptures. Men rich in virtue, lovers of beautifulness . . . . all these gained glory in their generations and were praised in their day.*" These words of the Holy Scripture are so strongly expressive of our church musicians that I cannot resist to quote them again. "Men rich in virtue and lovers of beautifulness." This is the secret of Church Music; it was written by men who were imbued with the Catholic spirit, and who used their gifts for the highest ends—the service of the Great Giver, and it is in this spirit that they have to be judged. I cannot conclude better than by quoting some words written by Beethoven in his diary after a special concert of his music got up in his honour during the great Vienna Congress. After the performance the Master went home and wrote: "Let everything that hath existence be devoted to the Most High, and become a sanctuary of Art. . . . . A small court, a little chapel, where my compositions shall be performed, to the praise of the Almighty, the Everlasting, the Eternal, and so let my days be passed." Noble sentiments of a truly Catholic heart!

APPENDIX.

A.

Principal Authorities consulted.

AMBROS. "History of Music."
BAINI. "Life of Palestrina."
BURNEY. "History of Music."
BELLASIS. "Memorials of the Life of Cherubini."
COUSSEMAKER. "History of Harmony in the Middle Ages."
CÆREMONIALE EPISCOPORUM.
GERBERT. "De Cantu et Musica Sacra."
HOPKINS. "On the Organ."
HAWKINS. "History of Music."
JAHN. "Life of Mozart."
LA MAITRAISE.
MAGISTER CHORALIS.
MATTHIEU. "Roland de Lattre."
NAUMANN. "History of Music."
POHL. "Life of Haydn."
RITTER. "History of Music."
STAINER. "Music of the Bible."
WESTMINSTER PROVINCIAL COUNCILS.
Various Articles in GROVES' "Dictionary of Music and Musicians."

&c., &c., &c.

B.

List of Masses recommended.

1.—FIRST CLASS RÉPERTOIRE.

Where obtainable.

ORDINARIUM MISSÆ. *Ratisbon Edition.*	Pustet, per Burns & Oates.
*BEETHOVEN. In C.	Novello.
*CHERUBINI. In A, C, E, F, G, and the two Requiems.	,,
HAYDN. *1, 2, 3, 4, 7 (except *Credo*), *16.	,,
MOZART. *1, *2, *3, 6, *7, *10, and Requiem.	,,
SCHUBERT. *F, G, B♭.	,,
GOUNOD, *" S. Cecile," " Du Sacre Cœur," " Des Paques." In G (T.T.B.B.).	,,
HUMMEL. In *D, *B♭, E♭.	,,
SILAS. In C.	,,
WINGHAM. In D.	,,
WESTLAKE. (S. Joseph.)	,,
PALESTRINA. " Missa Brevis."	Pustet, per Burns & Oates.
,, *" Æterna Christi munera."	,,
,, *" Papæ Marcelli."	,,
,, " Assumpta est."	,,
ORLANDO DI LASSO. " In Die Tribulationis."	,,
,, " Qual donna."	,,
VITTORIA. " O Quam gloriosum."	,,
Masses in PROSKE'S " Musica Divina."	,,

2.—SECOND CLASS RÉPERTOIRE.

ORDINARIUM MISSÆ. *Ratisbon Edition.*	Pustet, per Burns & Oates.
HAYDN. 7 (except *Credo*), and perhaps 1.	Novello.
MOZART. *2, *7, *10.	,,
RIGHINI. In *D.	Schott.
SCHUBERT. In G, B♭.	Novello.
HUMMEL. In *D.	,,
TOZER, In A♭ and D.	Cary.
FORRESTER. In E♭.	,,
VAN EYKENS. In A♭ and D.	Schott.
SHORT. " Mass of S. Joseph."	Novello.
PALESTRINA. *" Æterna Christi munera."	Pustet, per Burns & Oates.
,, " Missa Brevis."	,,
ORLANDO DI LASSO. " Missa Quinti Toni."	,,

3.—THIRD CLASS REPERTOIRE.

                                                                        Where obtainable.

ORDINARIUM MISSÆ. *Ratisbon Edition.* Pustet, per Burns & Oates.
GOUNOD. In C (Two Voices), in G (Three Voices). Per Novello.
TOZER. In A♭ and D. Two Voices.   Cary.
FORRESTER. In E♭.   ,,
MOLITOR. "S. Fidelis."   Pustet, per Burns & Oates.
   ,,   "Tota Pulchra."   ,,
   ,,   "SS. Angelorum."   ,,

The Masses marked * are included in a list recommended by a Commission of Ecclesiastics appointed by the Archbishop of Westminster shortly after the Fourth Provincial Council, and all of them are supplied by Messrs. Burns & Oates (Limited), 28, Orchard Street, London, W.

ADVERTISEMENT.

THE foregoing pages upon the History and Growth of Church Music appeared in the columns of the *Weekly Register*, and in answer to numerous requests on the part of his readers, the Author now presents them to the public in a permanent form. The Author is deeply sensible that he has treated the subject in a superficial manner, but his excuse is that he has had in view the interest of the general reader. This will also explain why his pen has sometimes wantoned in a merry mood. He gladly takes this opportunity of expressing his heartfelt thanks for the many kind letters he has received from all parts, and he is sensible that the flattering expressions which they contained can only be accounted for by the kindly and courteous hearts of the writers.

FEAST OF OUR LADY OF GOOD COUNSEL,
　　　　1887.

www.ingramcontent.com/pod-product-compliance
Lightning Source LLC
Chambersburg PA
CBHW020110170426

43199CB00009B/473